ALEX TREBEK

THE ANSWER IS ...

Reflections on My Life

SIMON & SCHUSTER

New York   London   Toronto   Sydney   New Delhi

Simon & Schuster
1230 Avenue of the Americas
New York, NY 10020

Copyright © 2020 by Alex Trebek, OC

First Simon & Schuster hardcover edition July 2020

SIMON & SCHUSTER and colophon are registered
trademarks of Simon & Schuster, Inc.

For information about special discounts for bulk purchases,
please contact Simon & Schuster Special Sales at
1-866-506-1949 or business@simonandschuster .com.

The Simon & Schuster Speakers Bureau can bring authors to your live event. For
more information or to book an event, contact the Simon & Schuster Speakers
Bureau at 1-866-248-3049 or visit our website at www.simonspeakers.com.

Interior design by Ruth Lee-Mui

Manufactured in the United States of America

7 9 10 8 6

Library of Congress Control Number 2020938903

ISBN 978-1-9821-5799-9
ISBN 978-1-9821-5801-9 (ebook)

A bit of potpourri for those who are hoping to become survivors.

INTRODUCTION

Of all the projects in my professional career, I am starting off on this one with the most serious misgivings. Over the past thirty years, I've been approached many times by publishers and writers to do an autobiography or consent to an authorized biography, but I've always turned them down. I've had no interest whatsoever. I didn't think I had anything pertinent to say to the world. And my life was not particularly exciting. I'm the typical product of my generation: a hardworking breadwinner who looks after his family; does all the repairs he can around the house; enjoys watching television; and thinks a simple dinner of fried chicken, broccoli, and rice is just fine, thank you very much. I've shown up to work at the same job for thirty-six years and have lived in the same house for thirty years. I respect and like my colleagues, and have a family that I dearly love. In this, I'm no different from many other people. I have never seen myself as anything special. That's why if you listen to Johnny Gilbert's announcement at the opening of *Jeopardy!*, I'm introduced as "the host" rather than "the star." I insisted on that when I took the job back in 1984.

But then early in 2019, all of that changed when I was diagnosed with stage IV pancreatic cancer.

At first, I was reluctant to share this news with the world. Basically, I'm a private person, but ultimately, I decided to do so because I wanted to stay ahead of the tabloids. I didn't want them printing or manufacturing all kinds of crap. But upon making the announcement, I quickly discovered there are millions of people out there who seem to care and who feel I have played an important part in their lives. I've received boxes and boxes of cards and letters from people around the world offering their support, encouragement, advice, and prayers. There is a very large glass display case inside the *Jeopardy!* studio that is filled with them. It's a humbling experience, but it is one that I thought deserved recognition. It made sense to respond to that outpouring of care, good wishes, and prayers. So I started to come around to this idea of a book.

I've got a very good friend whose opinion I respect a great deal. He's very intelligent, very insightful. As soon as he got wind of the fact that I was considering this project, he immediately fired a lot of questions at me.

"What's in it for you?" he asked. "I don't mean financially. I mean, what do you expect the benefits of a book will be for you? You've been in the public eye quite a bit for more than a year now, and the reaction has been very positive. Should you not be concerned that by revealing stuff from your past you might lose some of the goodwill that has been coming your way? Is this just an end-of-life reconciliation or settling of old scores? Is it basically what you did when you revealed your diagnosis: an attempt to stay ahead of the tabloids and any writer out there who is looking to publish an unauthorized biography that would rely on old clips and 'fake news'? Or is there more to it than that?"

See how bright he is?

That started me thinking: What *is* my goal here? Is there more to it than that? Like most people, I want to be liked. And I want people to know a little more about the person they have been cheering on for the past year. Sure, staying ahead of the tabloids is part of the reason also.

Once I made the decision to proceed, I quickly determined what this book would *not* be. This is not going to be a standard memoir. We're just hitting the highlights. It's a series of quick look-ins, revelations. It's an aperçu of Alex Trebek, human being. What is he like? What has he done? How did he screw up? Things like that.

Except for contributing the occasional *Jeopardy!* clue, I'm not a writer. And I especially do not feel comfortable writing about myself. When I met with Governor General of Canada David Johnston a couple of years ago, I got a chuckle out of him when I said, "Your Excellency, you and I have a lot in common. We're both from the Sudbury region. We've both played hockey with Phil Esposito. You have written twenty-two books, and I have *read* twenty-two books."

I've spent a career communicating verbally. So try to look at this as a conversation in which I get a chance to reveal a lot more about myself than I have ever done on *Jeopardy!* Some of what you will discover will undoubtedly surprise you. Some of it may even shock you. I'm going to do my best to recount things completely accurately, but I don't want people to hold me to that, and I don't want people coming back at me and saying, "You didn't get that right."

I will try to remember as much as I can, but the cancer, chemotherapy, and my age have taken a toll on me. My powers of recall have slowed. When I was younger, I had a great memory. I didn't forget anything. Now my memory is fading, and I feel I'm in the same boat as Mark Twain, who in his seventies said he remembered only things that never happened. If that occurs here, tough shit.

Revelation #1: Alex Trebek swears. (Though, as I'll explain a bit later, not as much as I used to.)

What Is . . .

THE NICKEL RANGE?

All right, let's start with something of significance. Approximately 1 billion, 850 million years ago, a large comet struck North America a mighty blow in what is now the province of Ontario, and, along with scattering masses of valuable industrial minerals as far away as Minnesota, left what is now called the Sudbury Basin, Earth's second-largest crater, eighty-one miles in diameter.

The large impact filled up with magma containing nickel, platinum, copper, gold, and other metals, making the area one of the world's major mining sites. My hometown of Sudbury lies just outside the southern rim and for many years was known as the Nickel Capital of the World.

My father, George Edward Terebeychuk, was this little Ukrainian immigrant who had earned his passage money to Canada mainly by playing violin at weddings and parties in his hometown of Nuyno. He arrived from Ukraine in the late 1920s. He was on a train bound for Manitoba to be a farm laborer, but when he got to Ottawa, he decided he didn't want to work on a farm, and he jumped off. He had a cousin, my uncle Mike, who lived in Toronto, and he touched base with him. Once Dad mastered the fundamentals of basic English and changed his last name to match his

The exterior of the Nickel Range Hotel, where I spent so much of my youth.

The rotunda of the Nickel Range Hotel.

cousin's, Mike got him a starting job in the kitchen at the King Edward Hotel, which was one of the two large first-class hotels in Toronto.

Dad knew nothing about cooking, but he got to like it, got good at it, and eventually, after a long apprenticeship, worked his way up to pastry chef. Then in the late thirties, he moved to the booming mining town of Sudbury. Ten years later, he was offered the job as cohead chef at the Nickel Range Hotel in Sudbury, and that brought about major changes in my life.

As I grew up, the kitchen became a second home to me, where I learned the value of the little things in life: the importance of punctuality; the rewards for hard, honest work; the pride of properly arranging tables and chairs; the camaraderie of a staff of waitresses and food preparers working together in harmony—although there was a time one of the meatcutters, obviously not happy with the way the waitress was placing her order, heaved a meat cleaver at her.

The hotel hosted all the main service clubs—Rotary, Lions, Kiwanis, Knights of Columbus—for luncheons and dinners and, because of the size of its ballrooms, many large receptions. I had two specific self-appointed duties at those events. When not portioning out the side dishes, I was in charge of slicing the large sheet cake for dessert.

Weddings—that's where I got to enjoy watching artistry in motion. Quite often Dad had to create and make the wedding cakes, and I never ceased to be amazed at his artistic talent: the delicacy of the flowers and leaves, the fronds, the architectural touches, all in a pure-white soft icing. I helped also. My job was to find as many empty Kodak Brownie film spools that would be iced and used as supports for the cakes' upper layers. Look at me, already a sous-chef at the age of eight.

Dad demonstrated his artistry and creativity in another way also. He and his co-chef, Jerry DeVilliers, used to prepare a special holiday treat for their friends. During the year they would accumulate all of the potato peelings and create a mash that would ferment for months in large bins in a basement storage room. Then, just before Christmas, they would set up a distillery. The first year was almost a disaster because the hotel's head of maintenance couldn't understand why the ice-making machines were always empty. He started to raise a fuss, but a bottle of the homemade vodka pacified him and he never complained again.

Oh, by the way, the meatcutter missed by a wide margin. But message sent and understood.

At that time, Sudbury had a population of around forty thousand. It has always amazed me that the entire city could fit inside the current Dodger Stadium. Why that stuck with me I've never known.

People would come into town to do business with the refineries or the mining operations. The Nickel Range Hotel was the prime quality hotel in the city, five stories high with a large lobby for public gathering and socializing. It was built in 1914, and by 1939 its reputation had grown considerably. Even though there were other contenders with worthy hotel names, Nickel Range seemed to truly reflect the spirit of the area, and it was there that the royal couple King George VI and Queen Elizabeth spent a night on their 1939 North American tour.

The hotel was very centrally located. It was a block and a half from the police station. Often the police officers on their morning patrol would stop at the hotel kitchen and ask George for a cup of coffee. In addition, they were arresting so many Eastern European mine workers, and nobody at the police station could speak Polish or Ukrainian or Russian, so they'd drag Dad—who spoke them all—out of the kitchen and over to the police station to translate so they could file proper papers on whoever it was they had arrested.

Dad would go to work at six thirty in the morning, do the breakfast until nine, then start preparing lunch. Lunch was from noon to one thirty. Then he had nothing to do from one thirty until the supper hours. So he'd come home and take a nap, and then go back to work around four thirty. He would get his work done pretty fast and would wind up going into the hotel tavern and having a beer. I'm not sure how he met my French Canadian mother, Lucille Lagace, but most likely it was because her brothers used to drink at the hotel and introduced them. Dad didn't speak a word of French but got along well with Mom's brothers and sisters, because they all drank beer.

Mom didn't drink or smoke. She was looking after her mother, who was not doing all that well. Mom was the baby of the family. There were originally fifteen children, but by the time she was born it was down to ten. I think her taking up with Dad might've been a way to rebel a little, and to try to get herself out of the house and out on her own. And Dad was happy because he had found a family. They cared deeply for each other.

They had to get married because Mom got pregnant. They

married in December 1939, and I was born in July—July 22, 1940, in a little shack of a house just behind my grandparents' home. There was no doctor. My aunt Eunice was the midwife. My mother went through thirty-six hours of labor before delivering me. She lived to be ninety-five and reminded me of this many times.

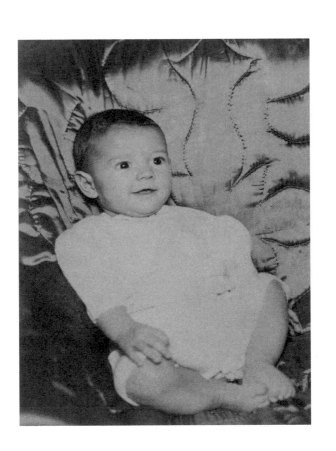

The Copper Cliff smelter in 1960.

What Is . . .

POLLUTION?

At this time, the outskirts of the city of Sudbury were very barren. Much of the timber had been forested to help rebuild Chicago after its great fire of 1871. Now the remaining vegetation was dying off. Sudbury's refineries became the scourge of North America. I remember hearing once that 80 percent of the people in Sudbury died of cancer. It was just part of life. We'd either get the choking hydrogen dioxide smoke from the refineries in Copper Cliff, which was a few miles away, or if the wind turned, we'd get the malodorous hydrogen sulfide fumes from the paper mill in Espanola, which was about fifty miles away. Either way, it was not the greatest atmosphere in which to grow up. But we didn't know any better. We just did our thing.

Showing off my left-slanting penmanship. That's my buddy Adelard Baker over my right shoulder at the very back of the class.

Who Is . . .

THE "LAST OF
THE BAD WOMEN"?

There were two primary schools side by side. One taught all their classes in English. My school, St. Louis de Gonzague, taught most of their classes in French. I was bilingual. My friends and I would speak both French and English. It depended on which students I was hanging around with at the time. A schoolmate, Adelard Baker, lived a block away from me, and we often walked the same path home. But he was a pain in the ass. He was a bit of a bully—always trying to lord it over everybody—pushing me and shoving me and teasing me. One day I got pissed and we got into a fight. I think it was a draw. But because I was so angry, I may have won the fight. But from that day on we became best friends, and he never teased me or bothered me again.

I was a good student in primary school. Got good grades. Little bit of a shit stirrer. The school was run by the Grey Nuns, and they did not like students who kidded around. In grade four, I fell in love with my teacher, Miss Charboneau. A gorgeous young lady. And then grade five was Miss L'abbé. She was either widowed or . . . I don't know. But she wasn't married. And she was even more beautiful—a tall, mature, statuesque brunette. She always came to class wearing a tailored suit and high heels. Adelard and I were the beneficiaries of a wonderful moment right before the Christmas break. On the last day of school, Miss L'abbé asked us if we would help carry her presents to her apartment. She lived along the same route that we took when we were going home. When we got to her apartment and unloaded everything, she rewarded each of us with fifty cents and a kiss on the lips. *On the lips.* I don't remember how I spent that fifty cents, but I lived off that kiss for weeks. I thought, *My God, she kissed me! I'm in love!*

In grade six, I got a nun who just didn't like me, and then in grade seven, I had a lady I referred to as Al Jennings, Last of the Bad Women—a big, tough old broad. She used to drink at the hotel with my dad, but that didn't soften her attitude toward me in class.

When I write—and my handwriting is pretty good—I slant to the left. She was teaching the students how to write properly and slant to the right. I wasn't buying any of that. So she whacked me a couple of times. I said, "Screw this." So I left school. I told my parents, "I'm not going back to Mrs. Jennings' class. She whacked me on the hands to get me to change my way of writing, and I don't like that."

I transferred to an English-speaking school in a different part of town. I lasted there about two months, because it just wasn't conducive to getting along with the other students. They didn't accept me. I was new and had come from a French-speaking school. So I transferred back to Mrs. Jennings' class at St. Louis. Strange, but she left me alone after that. Maybe she had been drinking enough with my dad in my absence.

The Answer Is . . .

TWO DOZEN EGGS

While Dad was at work, Mom was tending house and doing the things she enjoyed: sewing and cooking. Dad never cooked at home . . . and was never home for meals. He wasn't home for breakfast. He wasn't home for lunch. He wasn't home for dinner. I'd see him when he'd get home from work around eight thirty. Which was kind of good because if I had done something wrong and Mom was punishing me and telling me, "Wait until your dad gets home," I'd fake being asleep at eight thirty and Dad wouldn't bother me.

I used to love going to see him at the hotel kitchen. I'd spend a lot of time there. I'd go visit him, sit down, nibble on pies. Dad made the greatest shepherd's pie that I've ever had in my life. That was one of my favorites, with great gobs of beautiful brown gravy. I'd help out in the kitchen just to keep busy. I'd go into the corner where the big Hobart dishwashing machine was, and I'd run the dishwasher. I got a lot of satisfaction from operating a big piece of equipment. Or operating the big Hobart cake mixer. It was the size of a five-gallon vat.

I'd often quiz my dad, asking him for recipes. I asked him once how to make a chocolate cake, because I wanted to surprise Mom at home.

He said, "Well, first you take two dozen eggs . . ."

"What are you talking about, two dozen eggs? I just want to make a single cake."

He was used to making cakes for a hundred people at a lunch or dinner banquet. So I had to scale it down. And I made a good cake. He and Mom went out to dinner on a Saturday night. When they came home, I had made a spicy chocolate cake. Or maybe it was red velvet. Either way, they liked it.

Dad out back of the Nickel Range Hotel
in 1941, a year after I was born.

The Answer Is . . .

NECKTIES

After I was born, we lived with my grandparents for a while. They resided about a hundred feet away from us in a three-story house. And then we moved to an apartment right in the center of town. Unfortunately, not long after that, Mom was diagnosed with tuberculosis and had to go away to a sanitarium in Ontario. I was about nine or ten. My uncle Wilfred and my cousin Doris were diagnosed at the same time. So all three of them wound up at the same sanitarium in Gravenhurst, Ontario. They were in the hospital for the better part of a year and a half. I can't remember visiting my mother during that time. Maybe once, outside the hospital, but I don't recall them allowing children to go inside the hospital.

My grandmother and her second husband came to live in our apartment to look after us. My step-grandfather taught my dad how to play euchre and would continually beat him. Dad never got the hang of it, but he loved playing the game.

My grandmother cooked and tended house, which was kind of neat. She taught me how to make doughnuts. My job was to turn the doughnuts in the hot grease and then sprinkle the powdered sugar on top of them. She would save the doughnuts for company . . . but she always gave me the centers.

My grandmother was a great seamstress. She made clothes for me—trousers, jackets, and all that stuff. But one of her specialties was making Halloween costumes. She and one of my aunts used to work on those. They made this beautiful giant peacock outfit out of neckties. If you can imagine a bird covered in single multicolored overlapping feathers, then you get the picture. Every time she added a necktie, it became a feather. That was pretty spectacular. They used to rent out these costumes at Halloween. It was fun.

The whole family on my mother's side was very creative. All the boys were into construction, into painting, and it was fun watching them work on projects and learn just by observing. That has stayed with me all my life. I find that I learn more by watching than by taking a course.

What Is . . .

RHEUMATISM?

I had a good relationship with Barbara, my sister. I was her older brother. She looked to me for protection even when we were young. There was this one time, when we were living at my grandmother's house. I guess Barbara was five and I was seven. She was playing on a partially frozen river near the house. I saw her and her friends and chastised them.

"This is dangerous," I said. "You can't do this. I'll test the ice for you."

I tested the ice; it cracked, and I fell in.

Unfortunately, my directional judgment was not equal to my swimming abilities, and I surfaced on the other side of the river. A railway worker not too far away spotted me and came over to help me out and took me back home. We had to walk about a quarter mile to get to the bridge, and then we had to cross the bridge and then walk all the way back to the house. By the time I got to the house I was near frozen to death, soaking wet in winter clothing. My mother and my grandmother undressed me and tried to warm me up.

That was the beginning of about twelve years of terrible rheumatism—rheumatic pain behind my knees. I used to wake up crying in the night, and my mother or dad would get up and rub my legs with Sloan's liniment. And then one day, the pain just went away. Go figure.

My sister, Barbara, and me as toddlers.

Smiling for the camera with Mom and Barbara.

Who Is . . .

THE GREAT
GILDERSLEEVE?

After my mother returned from the sanitarium, we bought a two-story house. We rented out the upstairs to a Polish family, and we occupied the ground floor and the basement. On the ground floor was a kitchen, a bedroom for my parents, a living room, a dining room, and a porch that my dad covered and turned into a bedroom for my sister and myself. So we shared a long, lean bedroom. And it worked out fine.

I had my own little Philco radio. I would've been, what, more than six hundred miles away from Boston? And I was picking up stations like WBZ Boston and WBZA Springfield, AM and FM. I'd listen to *The Great Gildersleeve*, and I'd listen to *Lux Presents Hollywood*, and *Suspense* "brought to you by the Electric Autolite Company." It was fun. Those were my evenings. I'd fantasize. I'd listen to Dean Martin and Jerry Lewis, and Fibber McGee and Molly from 10:00 to 10:15 p.m. I was in hog heaven.

My sister didn't bother me. I was at one end of the porch. She was at the other. I wouldn't play it loud. It was right next to my pillow. I used to think to myself, *Barbara's at the other end. She's not too bothered. She'll go to sleep.*

The Answer Is . . .

RIDING A
STATIONARY PONY

Before we got that first house, we lived for a few years in Toronto. My dad had gone back to work at the King Edward Hotel to save for the down payment on a home.

In Toronto, my parents had a ton of Ukrainian, Russian, and Polish friends, and that made for some great celebrations, great parties. On Sundays everyone came over to our place. It was a three-story rented house with an in-ground gas pump in the backyard. I haven't thought about that gas pump in forever. Why do I remember that all of a sudden? We hosted because everyone else lived in apartments. There were lavish spreads of herring, dill pickles, cabbage rolls—and, of course, schnapps and vodka. Around the third glass of vodka, Dad would bring out his violin and start playing jigs. Poor Barbara went to the dining table once, wanting a glass of water. She grabbed a glass that looked like it contained water. It contained vodka. She sucked that up and then started screaming.

That house was where another of my life's many injuries and ailments occurred. I made myself a parachute, and I decided to try it out by jumping off the roof of the front balcony. How else are you going to try out a parachute? Jump from a park bench? No, you have to jump from a high place. A lot of people think I'm pretty sharp as the host of *Jeopardy!*, but when I look back on my life I did plenty of stupid things. Fortunately, that time, I just got a little bruised—messed up my knee a bit.

One day, a guy came through the neighborhood with a pony, charging kids to take their picture with it. Barbara got a photo—a beautiful shot. Then I came home. I had been out playing.

I said, "Oh jeez, you got your picture on a pony! I didn't get no picture!"

Mom responded, "Well, go get your picture taken."

I was wearing coveralls and I had dirt on my face, but it didn't matter. I climbed up and got my picture taken. The pony looked just about as sad as I did.

Look how regal the pony is in Barbara's hands. Look how sad it is in mine.

Back when quarterbacks used to throw the jump pass.

The Answer Is . . .

BOARDING SCHOOL

I never thought about whether we were poor. We existed, same as everybody else. My friends and I were all just lower-middle-class kids from lower-middle-class families. We played every sport: hockey, baseball, softball, basketball, football. I blew out my knee playing football. Some parents owned their homes. Some parents rented. We were all part of the same community.

Later on, after my family returned to Sudbury from Toronto, I became best friends with Maurice Rouleau. He was the one rich kid I knew. His father owned the Nickel Range Hotel and was my dad's boss. Maurice was incapable of constructing even one sentence without using the f-word as a noun, a verb, an adjective, or an exclamation point. He had the same birthday as mine, only he was one year older. But we were in the same class at school. We had a great time together. Every Sunday morning after Mass, Mr. Rouleau would drive his big Buick Roadmaster, come and pick me up, and take us all—me and Maurice and his two older brothers—to the local lake for swimming.

My dad didn't go to church. Mom did. She took me and Barbara. Or I went with the schoolkids. Or I went on my own. I went to Mass every Sunday.

In grade nine, Maurice went away to boarding school, the University of Ottawa prep school, run by the oblates of Mary Immaculate. He enjoyed it so much that every time he came home he'd be touting how great it was with the priests and all the other students. I started thinking, *Gee, that would be great.* I don't know how we managed it, but my dad pulled together some money and sent me there for grade ten. But it didn't work out quite as well as I had hoped.

My parents were two of the nicest people you'd ever want to run into. Easygoing. I've never met anybody who said they didn't like my mother or my father. They were just sweet people. They got along with everybody. They were kind. They were generous—to the extent that they could be generous. They never bad-mouthed anybody.

I mentioned earlier that my parents cared deeply for each other, but they were ill-suited. Dad was a smoker and a heavy drinker. Mom was a teetotaler, and she was brighter than he was. Divorce was almost unheard of in our community, but they separated, which caused me no end of grief. Somehow I thought it was my fault because they had been "forced" to marry.

I had been dealt a bad turn, and I thought, *I'm going to have to stand up for myself.* So I began acting out, and that didn't serve me well at the University of Ottawa prep school. I was unruly, so unruly they were going to throw me out my first year.

There was a priest named Father Roy. He was in his early thirties and had snow-white hair. He was a bit of a martinet and liked lording it over all the kids, and I wasn't buying any of that. So I took it upon myself to make life as miserable as possible for him. It got to be a little war between us. I would challenge. He would punish. I would find a way to retaliate. I enjoyed it. Years later, I returned to the school for a visit, and I ran into Father Roy. He was giving a tour to some young boys, and he said, "See that guy over there? He's the one who gave me all this white hair." He died not too long after that. Probably from meanness.

I won most of our set-tos. But Father Roy had the power. In early spring, I was hauled into the principal's office.

"We were going to throw you out," the principal said, "but it's close to the end of the year. So we're going to let you finish your school year. But we're not going to allow you to come back."

"Okay," I said.

But then that summer, I started thinking, *Jeez, this is not good.* So my dad and I went to Ottawa. From Sudbury to Ottawa is a 250-mile trip. He drove his new 1956 Ford Fairlane, which was the only car my dad could afford. And basically on bended knee we begged the principal to be allowed to come back. There were about 220 boarding students. They were split into an older group and a younger group. The younger boys were Father Roy's bailiwick. And he was an ass. Father Rosario Dugais looked after the older boys. He said he'd take a chance on me, and I never gave him cause to regret that decision.

What Is . . .

A MENTOR?

The rest of my stay at the University of Ottawa boarding school was paradise. I was a good student and a Mass server, and that put me in a very small dormitory with eighteen other guys. I think the reason we became Mass servers is because of the perks involved. We were first in line for the commissary. We could stay up a little later. We could leave the facilities in the evening. Instead of going to study hall, I could go to a movie theater, as long as I came back before the doors were locked. We worked hard for those privileges. Some mornings, I would serve two Masses at a time. There were two small altars next to each other, each with a priest performing a concurrent Mass. Boy, you had to be on your toes.

There was never any inkling of the kind of horror stories we hear about nowadays with priests and young boys and young girls. These were priests who were there to educate us. In my senior year, I had a spiritual adviser named Father Lorenzo Danis. He wasn't so much a spiritual adviser as a banker. I kept running short, so he would lend me money. And counsel me.

There were forty-four priests living in the building. Just down the hall from Father Danis was another of my favorites: "Big John" L'abbé, no relation to Miss L'abbé. He'd say Mass in about twelve minutes. He knew I didn't have much money, and when he'd notice I was hungry, he would give me some hosts and let me sip the wine. The other priests' rooms were very spartan, outfitted with little more than a cot, a pew, a desk, and perhaps a small radio. Big John's room had a sofa that opened into a bed. He had a Blaupunkt radio that could pick up the moon. He would sit there and read his breviary, smoking a Corona cigar and sipping cognac. He was enjoying the good life and taught me all about how to enjoy it as well.

He was my Latin teacher, and he created a special prize for me. There were already prizes for the first- and second-best grades in class. Those prizes were books. Just to help me, because I had never studied Latin before, and because Father L'abbé also knew that I had financial problems, he created a new prize for the student who showed the most improvement.

He said, "The winner is Alex Trebek, and he gets fifteen dollars in cash."

So I loved Big John. That was a sign that he cared for me. He was a good man.

Father Lorenzo Danis

The Answer Is . . .

AN IMPORTANT LESSON

A lesson in how to treat women and show respect for women oc-curred when I was in boarding school. After Dad and Mom had broken up and she had moved to the United States, he gave up his position as chef at the Nickel Range Hotel and took over a restau-rant in the small Northern Ontario municipality of Temagami. At the beginning it worked well because the Trans-Canada Pipeline was being put through Northern Ontario, and he had a lot of lunch business from the workmen—the welders and heavy-equipment operators. But when they had moved on to the next section of the pipeline, twenty miles up the road, and had found other places to eat, business started to slow down.

I was visiting him one holiday, and he wanted to move a sofa from one room to the next. He asked if I would help him.

"Sure," I said.

We tried to move the sofa, but it was too wide to go through the doorway. We stood it on end and tried to twist it in, but it was too deep to go through the doorway. We were going crazy. We were there half an hour trying to get this through the door.

Just then, Evelyn, one of his neighbors, who also happened to be the head waitress at the restaurant, walked by, took a quick look, and said, "Why don't you open the sofa into a bed?"

So we did. We laid it flat, stood it up on its edge, and slid it easily through the doorway. No problem at all.

My dad was pissed as all get-out. It was as if his manhood had been attacked. Me, I thought, *Holy smokes, she's brilliant. Women are sharp.* And that little incident colored my view of women from that day forward. I never underestimated women after that.

Dad and Evelyn, the wise coworker who rescued
us from our furniture-moving nightmare.

Who Is . . .

GEORGE ALEXANDER TREBEK?

By this time, I was going by "Alex." My given name is George Alexander Trebek. My dad was George Edward Trebek. I started going by Alex when I was in my early teens, just so that there would be no confusion when the phone rang and somebody said, "Is George there?" But throughout my life, within the family I was always referred to as "Sonny."

What Is . . .

MILITARY COLLEGE?

I couldn't afford college. I wasn't earning enough in the summer months, and Dad didn't have enough money to help. He had moved back to Sudbury after business had dried up at the restaurant in Temagami. So after I graduated from boarding school, I applied to the Regular Officer Training Program, or ROTP. This was a program administered by Canada's armed forces. If you were accepted, they paid your college for four years and then you had to serve for two years.

I received a letter instructing me to come to the Royal Canadian Air Force base in London, Ontario, for a couple of days of testing. There were written tests and lectures. Then they gathered all of us applicants in the mess hall. They divided us into groups of six, walked us over to one of the hangars, and led each group to a specific area. The groups were widely separated. Each area had a pile of stuff on the floor. There was lumber, ropes, pulleys, tarps, all kinds of ordinary tools and construction-type equipment—you name it.

We were then presented with a scenario. We were to imagine that each group was made up of prisoners enclosed in a three-sided reinforced concrete building. The fourth side was completely open to a twenty-foot-wide chasm hundreds of feet deep. Our mission was to use the pile of tools to escape and get to freedom on the other side of the chasm. We had an hour in which to accomplish this task. *Ready, set, go.*

The six of us in our group came up with idea after idea. "Maybe if we tie the boards together with the rope it will stretch across." It didn't. "Maybe if we try to build a teeter-totter and spring across." Nope, somebody's gonna die. "Maybe if we assemble a hoist with the pulleys and swing across." We worked and worked and worked. And agonized, really agonized over this. We didn't succeed in escaping. *Time's up.*

We went back to the mess hall to commiserate with the other teams and find out how many of them succeeded. None of them had. Not one. It turned out that the problem was unsolvable. So, what were they trying to accomplish? Simple. They wanted to see how the six members of each team interacted. They wanted to see if a natural leader would emerge—and if so, how would that leader treat the others in the group? Would he accept suggestions from them? Would he delegate authority? Would each person be given a specific task? How would the other members behave?

It would be nice for this book if I were to say I wound up being the leader of our group. I guess I could fudge it. There's nobody around who could say sixty years later, "Oh, no, Trebek wasn't the leader." The truth is, I cannot recall if I or anyone else assumed that role.

The exercise taught me a valuable lesson though: knowing what the goals are in life is very important. Sometimes we can make mistakes. Robert Frost took the road less traveled, and it worked out well for him, but that isn't true for everyone. And sometimes you have to understand what your true goal is in order to achieve it. And we don't always understand that.

Three weeks later I got word: *Congratulations, you have been accepted into the ROTP. You are hereby ordered to report to the Royal Canadian Air Force military academy college in Saint-Jean, Quebec.* What? That wasn't what I had signed up for. I wanted to attend college at the University of Ottawa. I had just fallen in love with Eleanor Mans, the cousin of one of my friends. I didn't want to go six hundred miles away from Sudbury. But my government had instructed me to report, so I did.

We got off the buses and were met by the senior cadets, who were immediately a bunch of dicks. Intent on making life miserable for the new class, they demanded we form lines facing the sun and started ordering us about.

"You're wearing sunglasses? Cuff links? Get rid of them. No jewelry should be visible."

I had shown up wearing the current style of sport jacket. It had two buttons, but you never buttoned both.

"Fasten that other button," they said.

It put a bulge in the jacket and made it look dorky. I soon realized that the individuality of one Alex Trebek was quickly disappearing.

After making us stand in the hot sun for a good forty-five minutes, they ordered us inside to get our room assignments and bedding. Then they taught us how to make the bed so that a silver dollar would bounce on it. I made mine.

"Who made this bed?" one of the seniors said. "Whose bed is this?"

"It's mine, sir," I said.

"It's perfect. You did a very good job."

"Thank you, sir."

"Now tear it up."

"Wait a minute, why do you want me to tear it up?"

"No back sass," he said, tearing the bed up for me. "On the floor and give me ten."

"But wait a minute, the other guys didn't do as good of a job—"

"Make it twenty."

I felt like saying, "You son of a bitch. I did it right the first time and you're going to get me to do it again?" Instead, I got down on the floor, did my push-ups, then made the bed again.

None of this was what I had anticipated or bargained for. On the third day, they were giving haircuts, and that's what put me over the edge. In those days hairdos were big. I had a good head of hair— a sort of pompadour with a ducktail in the back. I'd be damned if I was going to let them shave it off. I said, "I've had enough of this crap. I can't deal with these yo-yos who are just throwing their weight around for whatever reason."

I went to see the vice commandant. I told him I had never wanted to go to military college. I wanted to attend university. He was very soft-spoken, very kind, very understanding.

"It's a big move," he said.

"I'm not sure it's for me," I replied.

"I understand, but you scored very high in the testing, and you demonstrated leadership qualities we want in the air force. Why don't you go back to your quarters, think on it overnight, then come back tomorrow and let me know your decision."

No way was I going to let the military
buzz this lush head of hair.

So I did. I slept on it, and in the morning I went back and told him I had made up my mind. I didn't want to stay. That's when I discovered the bad cop side of him.

"If you don't have the guts to stick this out, you're not the kind of person we want in our military. Get your gear together, see the sergeant outside, and get your passage back home."

I called my dad.

"Dad, I'm leaving military college."

"What happened? Did they throw you out?"

"Nope, I'm just leaving."

That was around early morning. By the time I arrived home in Sudbury around eleven thirty at night, my dad had managed to consume a bottle of rye and greeted me at the train station a little under the weather. He gave me a big hug.

"Don't worry, Sonny," he said. "Everything will be all right."

And it was.

What Is . . .

MY FAVORITE MOVIE?

I have always loved movies. When I went to boarding school, I started keeping a diary. After three weeks the diary consisted of nothing but titles of the movies I had seen. In college, the day before a big economics exam, I went out with my buddies to a "horror-thon" at one of the local theaters. Five horror movies. We walked into the theater around dinnertime and didn't walk out until one in the morning. I stayed up for another couple of hours cramming for my economics exam. I got my worst grade of any exam I took in college. I realized, *Maybe I shouldn't go see five movies the night before my final.*

Any movie about fathers and sons blows me away. It can be the simplest of movies, but if there's a father-son relationship in it, it just registers very strongly with me. The movie *How Green Was My Valley* is my favorite. I've seen it, I don't know, a dozen times. And it always brings a tear to my eye.

There's one scene in particular that always gets me. It's at the dinner table where the eldest sons are all up in arms because they want to form a union. The father, played by Donald Crisp, says:

"You will not make me a plank for your politics. I will not be the excuse for any strike."

43

"But if they learn they can do things like that to the spokesman,
   what will they try and do to the men?"

"We will see . . . Be silent now, finish your supper."

"But father—"

"Enough now."

"It is not enough."

"Owen, hold your tongue until you have permission to speak."

"I will speak against injustice anywhere with permission or without it."

"Not in this house."

"In this house and outside, sir."

"Leave the table."

"I will leave the house."

"For the last time," the father says, "sit down . . . finish your supper. I will say no more."

"We are not questioning your authority, sir, but if manners prevent our speaking the truth, we will be without manners."

"Get your clothes and go," he says.

And they do.

The youngest son, played by Roddy McDowall, is the only one
left at the table. He looks at his dad and starts dropping his knife
and fork on his plate to make noise. He knows he's not supposed
to talk, but he's letting his dad know he's there. His father, without
looking up, just says, "Yes, I know you're there, my son."

And that . . . that says about all you need to say about the love
that exists between a father and son. You don't have to explain it.
You don't have to go into detail. It's just a quiet little sign.

My dad was like that. He let me know in subtle ways. They weren't subtle to him. They were just quiet. He was not an educated man. He was not particularly bright. He was just all heart. He didn't understand nuances of caring. He just poured out his love for me. He once said, "Barbara's the baby, but Sonny's the one." It didn't matter what I did, I was never a disappointment to him. Leaving the military academy when we had no money didn't matter. He was just happy to welcome me home. I never let him down no matter what I did.

What Is . . .

REBELLION?

My mother left Sudbury and moved to Detroit, where two of her sisters lived. She got a job working as a governess for a family that had two kids. And unbeknownst to me, she was pregnant. When she and my father broke up, she took up with a gentleman in Sudbury, and he got her pregnant. He didn't want to marry her, so she left town and had the baby—a boy—and gave him up for adoption. I didn't know anything about it. I didn't know I had a half brother until shortly after I started hosting *Jeopardy!* He and I have communicated over the years, but we are not close.

Because of the way things happened, I had kind of a resentment for my mother. But we settled all that before she died—long before she died.

What Is . . .

GRADE THIRTEEN?

After I came back to Sudbury from military college, I had no money. For a couple of months I stayed in a tiny room in the annex of the Nickel Range Hotel, where Dad worked. It was just across the hall from another tiny room where he would change into his work clothes each day.

Then I went to stay with an uncle and aunt—my mom's brother and his wife. Most of their kids had moved out, and they had an empty room. It was barely big enough to fit a bed and a desk. There wasn't even enough room for my tape recorder, which I had to keep in the kitchen. My parents knew how much I loved listening to the radio, and they had bought me this tape recorder to tape music and programs. It was a huge machine—not your five-dollar cheapo. Taping music off the radio was always frustrating because so many of the announcers would talk over the orchestral vamp leading into the lyrics. If Frankie Avalon didn't come into the song for twelve seconds, the announcer would talk that entire time. I hated that.

"Shut up!" I'd yell at the radio. "I want the whole song!"

Of course a few years later I would end up doing the same thing when I worked as a disc jockey for the Canadian Broadcasting Corporation (CBC).

I always liked wearing suits, even before
my career as a television host.

THE ANSWER IS . . .

My uncle Ben would laugh at how upset I'd get. I could always make him laugh. While I was living with him and my aunt, he had thyroid surgery, and when I went to see him in the hospital he said, "Sonny, don't you dare make me laugh or I'll kill you!" It hurt too much for him to laugh.

Again, I didn't have money to go to college, so I went back to Sudbury High for one more year. Ontario had what they called "matriculation year." It was grade thirteen, or the equivalent of first-year university. My favorite subject was geography. I also liked geometry. Anything with a *g*. Geography, geometry . . . and girls.

The University of Ottawa boarding school had been all boys. Back in Sudbury, having narrowly escaped getting my hair buzzed off by the military, I started back up with my new girlfriend, Eleanor. I took her to the Sudbury High prom. Unfortunately, right before the dance she moved with her parents to North Bay, Ontario, which was about ninety miles away from Sudbury. Using Dad's Ford, I had to drive ninety miles to go get her and ninety miles back. I had to leave Sudbury at two in the afternoon to pick her up. Luckily, she had arranged for another ride home. With Eleanor living so far away, our relationship soon fizzled.

I was very shy with girls. I was not forward at all. You would have to throw me into a girl's arms and she would have to accept me willingly for anything to happen. I was not about to make the first move. But after Eleanor, I did fall in love with another girl. I took her to the movies; we held hands, but it wasn't until after two features, three cartoons, and a newsreel that I finally got the nerve to kiss her.

After returning to Sudbury, I started hanging around again with

Maurice Rouleau, my friend who swore a lot and whose dad owned the Nickel Range Hotel. He was also in grade thirteen at Sudbury High. The last week of school he got me in big trouble. It was our final gym class, and all the guys were excited. They thought they'd be funny, and so they grabbed some newspapers and magazines that were lying around in the locker room, got them soaking wet, mashed them up into balls, and threw them against the ceiling, where a lot of them stuck.

The gym teacher told the vice principal, Mr. Costigan, about this. So just before we were to leave class that day, Mr. Costigan came in and said, "I heard what you guys did this morning in the shower rooms. Those of you who were responsible stay here. We're gonna go clean up your mess. And the rest of you can leave." Well, I hadn't been involved, and so I started to leave.

"Hey, Trebek," Maurice called out, "you were there too."

I responded in French with a mild obscenity. It did not occur to me that Mr. Costigan spoke French fluently. He came charging over three rows of benches, grabbed me by the armpits, lifted me up, and pushed me so hard against the blackboard that dust was coming out of all the cracks. Even though I was innocent, I wound up going with the other guys to clean up the mess.

As we were walking to the locker room, I said to Maurice, "You know I wasn't there. Why the hell did you tell him that?"

"I was just fucking with you," he said.

At graduation, my homeroom teacher, Kenny Gardner, took me aside. Kenny had once told students in another class, "There's a kid in my homeroom, sits at the back of the class, doesn't say a word. But in discussions, if the students are ever stumped and can't come up with the answer to a question I'm asking, I'll point to him and he gives me the correct response. He's just a good student. Well-behaved." That had gotten back to me, and it meant a lot, because I was mostly known for joking around in class, though never in a disruptive way. Years later, when I started hosting game shows, those words would take on added significance—seem prophetic even. Yet something Kenny told me that day at graduation would have an even greater impact on me.

He said, "Alex, you've had a good year. Do me a favor. Never lose your love of life."

I was just torn apart by that line. Because somebody had finally recognized what I thought I was about.

What Is . . .

MY FIRST U.S. JOB?

I visited America a few times to see my mother and her sisters, my aunts Eunice and Alice. I'd take a Greyhound bus to Detroit, where Eunice would drive us around in her Cadillac convertible. I'd think, *Damn, Aunt Eunice really knows how to live!* She was involved with a married man who worked at Tiger Stadium, so I got to attend a lot of Tigers games.

My mother's work as a governess then took her to Cincinnati. She had been hired by the singer Nancy Reed Kanter—who'd toured Europe with Benny Goodman's band and had appeared on TV variety shows such as *The Frank Sinatra Show*—and her husband, Joseph Kanter, who was a developer. The summer I was eighteen, Mom got me a job in Cincinnati working on the maintenance crew of an apartment complex owned by Mr. Kanter. The Midwestern humidity was awful. I'd go back to my apartment in the complex for lunch, and I would be so thirsty I'd drink a gallon of lemonade. My apartment was even more barren than the rooms of the boarding school priests. I had no furniture except for a bed and a television set. My dresser was a cardboard box that the toilet paper came in.

At work, I mopped halls and repacked garbage cans. People are terrible at filling garbage cans. They'll see six big cans and fill each one halfway instead of loading three of them full. I spent much of that time leafing through the magazines people would throw out: *Time*, *Life*, *Newsweek*. As a result, I got fired before the summer was over.

The best part of that summer was a girl I dated who drove a red 1958 Chevrolet Impala convertible. We would make the short drive over the Ohio River to Southgate, Kentucky, to catch shows at the Beverly Hills Supper Club, which—before burning down in a tragic 1977 fire—drew nightlife acts from around the country and was famous for giving young Dean Martin his start as a blackjack dealer.

Later, Mom lived in Florida with my aunts, and I would visit her down there. America was a whole new world of affluence to me.

Who Is . . .

ST. THOMAS AQUINAS?

In America, in the early sixties, we were also starting to see the political and social upheaval that would dominate the country through the decade. None of that was happening in Ottawa. After graduating from Sudbury High, I returned there to attend the University of Ottawa. I had no money, and neither did Dad, so I had to pay my way through school with part-time jobs, such as processing tax forms for the Canadian Revenue Agency. I still kept in touch with Big John and Father Danis, and they looked out for me.

Father Danis would lend me money and take me out to dinner. But he refused to wear his vestments in public. He wanted to blend in but he would wear the most god-awful Hawaiian shirts you could imagine. He figured, *Nobody's going to know I'm a priest.* So he'd have on his black pants, his black shoes, and a Hawaiian shirt. In Ottawa. In October. Yep, nobody's gonna know.

Growing up, I wanted to either be a pilot, a doctor, or the prime minister of Canada. Once I got to college, I realized I could be a pilot no matter what occupation I was pursuing. All I had to do was take flying lessons. So I pushed that aside. I did briefly consider going into medicine. Father Danis had set up the faculty of medicine at the University of Ottawa, and he was urging me to go that route. But working part-time to pay for school, I was starting to get tired of going to class. That made me push medicine aside, and once I discovered broadcasting, I abandoned any political aspirations.

I majored in philosophy—specifically Thomistic philosophy, based on the teachings of St. Thomas Aquinas. We studied ethics, criteriology, and metaphysics. I did not choose this major because I was a brooding teenager plagued by existential quandaries. I chose it out of convenience. The classes were from nine to noon and allowed me to work in the afternoons and evenings in order to pay for school. I didn't know what I wanted to do after I graduated, and philosophy seemed like a good subject to pursue until I figured out where I was and what I wanted to do with my life.

I'm glad I studied philosophy. I think that a philosophical outlook will help you no matter what you are doing. Philosophy helps you in terms of acknowledging some sense of perspective in your life and in the world around you. I have always tried to approach life with what I call the "reasonable-man attitude." If you have some sense of perspective, you are not likely to get too high or too low.

And in one way, studying philosophy in Latin did help prepare me for a career as a quiz show host: if nothing else, it taught me how to pronounce *Nietzsche*.

That's me in the middle of the back row. Larry Bird I was not.

The Answer Is . . .

TEAMWORK

I played varsity basketball in my senior year at the University of Ottawa. Once, we went down to Utica, New York, to play an American team. We were scheduled to play them Friday night and Saturday night. Friday night they beat us by about forty points. They were giants. Our tallest guy was six foot three. We were pissed.

We said, "We'll show them tomorrow. We'll do a lot better. Might not win, but we'll do better."

The next night they beat us by a bigger score.

I was six feet tall and played point guard. I had a good set shot, but I wasn't the best player on the team. I was the one who settled everybody down, kept them even-tempered, didn't let them get too despondent. You always need somebody like that on a team, and those were traits that would serve me well in my professional career, which was just about to begin.

Getting started with the Canadian Broadcasting Corporation.

What Is . . .

EXPERIENCE?

I first tried to get a job in radio when I came back to Sudbury for grade thirteen. I was in need of a job, and I had won a public-speaking contest in grade three. I don't know why that stuck with me, but I figured, *You speak well, so maybe you could announce.*

The station manager I auditioned for politely rejected me. "Well, you're very, very young," he said, "but you've got a good voice."

Then in my junior year at university, I auditioned for a private radio station in Ottawa. They liked what I did, yet they wouldn't hire me. "We think we're one of the top stations in the country," they said, "and it wouldn't look good if we hired somebody who has absolutely no experience. Go get some experience, and then maybe we'll consider hiring you."

I thought, *That's a stupid argument to make.* "Hey, you did a good job, but we're not gonna hire you because we're only hiring people with experience." *What does it matter, for crying out loud? If I can do the job just as well as somebody with experience . . . the fact that you hired me, does that make you look bad? Doesn't it make you look good that you discovered a fresh talent? You should say, "We found somebody new! He's good!"*

But they didn't see it that way.

Maybe my rebellious streak kept me from taking no for an answer. That same summer I applied for an opening at the CBC. I still have the audition tape. I wore a nice herringbone suit and carried a pipe. I was trying to look mature while I did my best Walter Cronkite–type introduction. They had me read from a script and do some ad-libbing.

I got the job. It was a temporary summer position. Then over the Christmas holidays, I went to them and said, "Hey, you've got a lot of married guys on staff who are going to want to be home with their families. Why don't you put me on temporary for the Christmas holidays?" And they did.

The radio station was on the top floor of the Château Laurier hotel. So they got me a room and had me sign on the station at 6:00 a.m., work all day, sign off at midnight, and sign it back on at 6:00 a.m. They were happy with the work I did. In February they came to me like in *The Godfather*, with an offer I couldn't refuse.

"We have two full-time openings on our staff, and we'd like you to have one of them."

"Sure," I said, "as long as I can finish my school year." This was my last semester of university.

"Okay." They hired me as a staff announcer and arranged a schedule that allowed me to attend class in the morning and work in the evening. I enjoyed the work, and I was good at it. To be honest, I didn't have anything particularly complex to do. Mostly it was local news and weather. And the stockyard report: "Canners and cutters, so much a pound." Every night just after midnight, I'd sign off by reading a passage from the Bible. Then some mornings I'd be back in early to sign on at 6:00 a.m. Then I would go to class from 9:00 a.m. to noon. But because I was so invested in the job, my marks kept getting worse and worse, and I ended up graduating in the fall rather than in the spring.

Nope, still no mustache yet.

What Is . . .

MUSIC HOP?

I worked in Ottawa for two years before being transferred to CBC national headquarters in Toronto. They transferred me because, one, I was bilingual—the only bilingual announcer on staff—and two, they had an opening for me on a television program called *Music Hop*. It was a weekly teenage music show that predated *Hullabaloo* and *Shindig!* in the United States. We had a variety of musical guests, such as Gordon Lightfoot, David Clayton-Thomas (who'd later become lead singer for the band Blood Sweat & Tears), and Lorne Greene singing his hit "Ringo." The show was quite popular, and it gave me my first taste of "celebrity." People would occasionally come up to me on the street and tell me how much they enjoyed the program—though being Canadian, they were always courteous and apologetic for intruding.

I had already done some live TV while I was in Ottawa. But no matter how much experience you have, live TV is always challenging. If you mess up on live TV—which I did—you had better learn how to redeem yourself. Once, on *Music Hop*, I was standing at home base and introduced a mystery guest named "Mr. Voice." He was, in fact, *me*. It was a character I was to play in disguise. I threw to the band, who broke into a vamp intro. While they were doing that, the producers hurriedly gave me a mask and a cowboy hat. Unfortunately, they gave me the cowboy hat first, and I couldn't get the mask over the hat. So I was a bar and a half late coming into the song. And I'm not a singer. But I caught up and got it done.

Afterward, the three backup singers came over to me and said, "For a non-singer you did really well. You saved the number."

The director said the same thing at the end of the show.

"You did a great job," he told me.

To which I replied: "Mr. Voice has sung his last song."

Messing up on live TV taught me an important lesson about show business: learn to laugh at yourself.

On the set of *Music Hop*.

Interviewing Gordon Lightfoot.

The Answer Is . . .

PRACTICAL JOKES

There's an old joke about television newscasts: because you're shot from the waist up only, it doesn't matter if you're wearing pants. One day I was doing the news and one of my colleagues, an older announcer, decided he was going to poke fun at me. He finished reading the local community news, then said to the viewers at home, "Take a look over here . . ." The cameraman, who was in on it, panned around so the audience could see behind the news desk. And there I was: jacket, shirt, tie, shorts, and flip-flops.

My colleagues and I always used to play jokes like that on one another. When I got transferred to Toronto, one of the top announcers there was a big drinker. The CBC had two radio networks—the Dominion Network and the TransCanada Network. He'd do the national news on one; I'd do the national news on the other. We'd do it every hour from 6:00 p.m. until 11:00 p.m. It was a fifteen-minute report, so we'd have nothing to do from fifteen minutes after the hour until the top of the next hour. The Four Seasons Motor Hotel was right across the street from the station. They had a bar, so we'd go over there. I wasn't a drinker, but this colleague of mine was. Five times a night we'd make the journey from the station to the hotel bar and back. By the time we got to the ten and eleven o'clock newscasts, I'd often have to steady him to keep him from getting run over by the traffic coming down Jarvis Street.

And yet it was the most amazing thing: he'd get on the air and you would not know anything was amiss. He could be wobbly on his way to the studio, but on the air he was the perfect announcer, rock solid. So we delighted in trying to break him up. Once, when he was on the air, we opened the studio door and rolled in an empty seven-inch tape spool. We rolled it with a flick of the wrist so that it would spin. As the spool began to slow, it started making more and more noise, until it flattened on the ground. And when it flattened, he finally cracked. He switched off his mic for a moment and came out and cursed us. That was the only time I ever saw him break on the air.

Other guys would do the same thing to me. Once, I was doing a television newscast and a guy mooned me on the other side of the glass. I just barely kept it together. I can't believe that we did all those things in those days. Nowadays you wouldn't dare behave that way. But, hey, this was Canada. We're out to have a good time, eh?

What Is . . .

PUNCTUALITY?

Everyone who works on *Jeopardy!* knows that I am early for everything. If there is a meeting at eight in the morning, I'm there from ten until eight. If I'm not where I need to be ten minutes early, I consider myself late. It is a sign of respect for the job—that you want to do it well and not leave anything to chance.

I learned the importance of punctuality in grade eight, when my dad got me a summer job as a bellhop at the Nickel Range Hotel, where an average tip was ten cents and a big tip was twenty-five cents. The weekend before my first day of work, we had a class trip to celebrate the end of the school year. We traveled from Sudbury to Ottawa to Montreal to Quebec City, then back to Sudbury. I didn't get much sleep those three days, and mostly it was on the bus. So I came home that Sunday night and went straight to bed. The next morning, I woke up and it was eleven. I was three hours late for my first shift at the hotel.

Mr. Rouleau—the owner of the hotel and father of my friend Maurice—went to my dad and said, "George, Sonny is not here. He was due for work at eight o'clock." So the phone call came from

Dad, and I rushed down to work. That day I vowed I'd never be late to a job ever again.

Here's an example of how seriously I took this vow. When I first started for the CBC in Toronto, in addition to my weekly job hosting *Music Hop*, I signed on to the radio station at 5:00 a.m. and hosted a morning show until 9:00 a.m. I was younger then. I figured if I took a short afternoon nap, I could go see movies and plays and concerts in the evening, then as long as I got to bed by 1:00 a.m. I'd be okay to get up at 4:15 a.m. and ready for the sign-on, where I would review those events. And, since I lived three blocks from the station, it was a quick commute.

Just in case, the producer had me record a safety tape that would cover the first half hour. There was some music and me doing some generic vamping: "Welcome to a new day here at CBC." If I didn't show up, the engineer would put on the tape and call me, then I'd rush over and pick up off the tape.

"Don't worry about it," I told him, remembering the lesson I'd learned at the Nickel Range Hotel. "I'm never going to be late. I'll always get up."

The producers and the crew members weren't so confident. They started a pool as to how long it'd be before I overslept.

I started the show in September, and sure enough, in mid-November I woke up at three minutes after five.

"Holy shit!" I said. I jumped out of bed. "That's it! I'm going to lose the bet!"

I quickly got dressed, and I realized the engineer hadn't called me. I flipped on the radio, but the safety tape wasn't playing.

"Why aren't they playing the tape?" I said. "That's the reason we did it. It was supposed to cover me!"

I ran like mad those three blocks to the station. As I'm running up the stairs to go into the building, I glanced behind me.

Jeez, I thought, *there's a lot of traffic for five o'clock in the morning.*

Just then, another CBC staff member was walking out.

"Hi, Alex," he said. "You working tonight?"

"What?" I said. Only then did I realize what happened. This was during winter, when it gets dark early in Toronto. I had taken a nap in the afternoon. It was 5:00 *p.m.* I was embarrassed as all hell. But I was not late for work.

While my colleagues at *Jeopardy!* have all come to appreciate and adopt my insistence on punctuality, at home it's a different story. Dealing with family who are not of this same belief can drive you crazy. I'll tell them, "We're leaving at five." Which to me means ten minutes to five. But they take it literally.

"You said we're leaving at five! You didn't say be ten minutes early!"

I've done a lot of sitting and waiting in cars for my wife and children.

The Answer Is . . .

ENCOURAGEMENT

While I was hosting *Music Hop*, I was also hosting my first quiz show: *Reach for the Top*. Teams of high school students from across Canada would play against one another for prizes such as books and scholarships.

I learned an important lesson about being a good quiz show host from working on *Reach for the Top*. Teenagers are very sensitive. They have fragile egos. I know this from now having raised two of them—and having been one myself. A lot of the contestants on *Reach for the Top* were bookish, introverted types and especially delicate. They were very nervous about being on live television in front of an entire country. So if they got an answer wrong, I was careful not to be too harsh. I didn't want to embarrass them. Instead, similar to my role on the University of Ottawa basketball team, I would do my best to reassure them and encourage them to keep trying.

I do the same thing to this day on *Jeopardy!* If you watch the show on a regular basis, you'll notice that often when a contestant guesses wrong, I'll respond gently, "Oh, you were so close. You were probably thinking of . . ." Or I'll say, "You were just a few letters off. An easy mistake." I want to keep them from getting down

My first quiz show.

on themselves and going into a funk for two or three minutes and falling completely out of the game. During a taping just the other day, in fact, we had a contestant who got himself in the red real fast. He was negative $2,300. And I just said a couple of encouraging things, and all of a sudden, in Double Jeopardy! he turned it around. By the end of Double Jeopardy! he was right up there and vying for the win.

I'm not doing this simply to be kind. I'm doing it because the more competitive contestants are, the better it is for the game. I want to keep everyone in contention. I want them to realize that it was a momentary lapse, and we all have those. Though I don't say it directly, I'm attempting through my tone and phrasing to convey the message: *Don't worry about it. Just look ahead to the next question. You didn't get here by accident. You passed the test. You deserve to be here. These categories maybe don't line up with your areas of expertise. But you're bright. Keep your head up. Move forward. Keep going.*

It's an approach I have developed over time, and it all began on *Reach for the Top*.

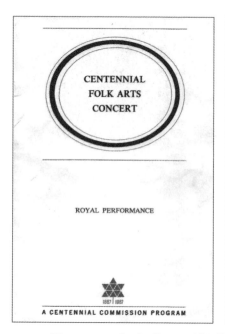

**CENTENNIAL
FOLK ARTS
CONCERT**

ROYAL PERFORMANCE

1867 | 1967

A CENTENNIAL COMMISSION PROGRAM

PERFORMING GROUPS

In order of appearance

Master of Ceremonies — ALEX TREBEK

OTTAWA	THE CONCORDIA GERMAN MALE CHOIR
SASKATOON	YEVSHAN UKRANIAN DANCERS
QUEBEC CITY	LES FANTAISISTES
LORETTEVILLE, QUEBEC	KABIR-KOUBAT INDIAN DANCERS
VANCOUVER	THE HIGHLAND LASSIES
OTTAWA	ROBIN MOIR — WITH THE CONCORDIA GERMAN MALE CHOIR
TORONTO	CHINESE COMMUNITY DANCERS
ST. JOHN'S, NEWFOUNDLAND . .	THE NEWLAND SINGERS
HALIFAX	JOHN ALAN CAMERON
CHARLOTTETOWN . .	KEN CAMPBELL AND ED DOIRON
MONTREAL	THE MOROMAGUY DANCERS
OTTAWA	THE FIVE D — ROCK GROUP
QUEBEC CITY	LES FANTAISISTES
TORONTO	THE BUTLER IRISH DANCERS
WINNIPEG	ISRAELI DANCERS
TORONTO	KALEV ESTONIAN GIRL GYMNASTS

Musical Accompaniment by

THE ROYAL CANADIAN AIR FORCE TRAINING COMMAND BAND

DIRECTOR OF MUSIC — FLIGHT LIEUTENANT J. WOODS

PIT ORCHESTRA, DIRECTOR — MR. BERTHOLD CARRIÈRE

The program for the Centennial Folk Arts Concert Royal Performance.

The Answer Is . . .

A LESSON IN HUMILITY

Soon my job responsibilities at the CBC increased. I covered sporting events such as the Canadian Triple Crown of racing, tennis championships, and curling tournaments. I introduced the Toronto Symphony Orchestra and the Canadian Ballet. One time Rudolf Nureyev performed with the ballet. I stood in the wings with the young ballerinas watching him, all of us marveling at his grace and athleticism as he pirouetted effortlessly around the stage. As he drew closer to us, though, we were all shocked. With each spin, he would say, "Fuck shit! Fuck shit! Fuck shit! Fuck shit! Fuck shit!" It was soft enough that the audience didn't hear but loud enough to scandalize the young members of the company.

In addition to Nureyev, I got to meet a lot of celebrities: Ed Sullivan, the Canadian comedy duo Wayne and Shuster, and George Burns. I met George when he was brought in by the CBC to introduce the fall programming lineup—what these days are called "upfronts." Shortly after he said, "I went up there to Toronto to introduce their fall campaign. Canadians are weird. I'd be telling a joke, and the audience would start to laugh at the wrong spot. They would laugh early. Then I finally discovered that they're poor up there. They can't afford to write on only one side of the cue card.

So they had written on both sides of the cue card, and the audience was reading the other side of the cue card with the punch line and laughing before I got to it."

My most memorable celebrity encounter during that time was in 1967. It was Canada's centennial year. I was the only bilingual announcer on staff, so they assigned me to host the CBC's big extravaganza on Parliament Hill. It was a two-hour variety show featuring all kinds of performers. They had singers. They had dancers. They had musicians. They had acrobats. There were also many dignitaries, foremost among them Queen Elizabeth and Prince Philip.

At the end of the show, all the performers lined up onstage, and Queen Elizabeth and Prince Philip made their way down the line, greeting each of them. As the host, I was at the end of the line. The Queen got to me and said, "Good show. Please tell me your name, and where you are from." And as I began answering her, I couldn't help but notice that she glanced over her shoulder, just for a second, to see where Prince Philip was. Now, normally in public the Queen has Prince Philip one or two steps behind her, and she will not leave the stage until he is accompanying her. Only this time he wasn't one or two steps behind. He had paused fifty feet back and was chatting up the Kalev Estonian gymnasts—a group of twenty-year-old blond girls in electric-blue leotards. So the Queen was stuck talking to me for four or five minutes. You're not supposed to lead the conversation with the Queen. She loved horses, and once she found out I was hosting the Canadian Triple Crown of racing, we spent much of our discussion on that. Finally, after several minutes of conversation, Prince Philip showed up and said, "Good show," shook my hand, and off they went.

That night my phone was ringing off the hook. I was getting calls from friends and relatives from all over the country saying, "Oh my God, what happened? You were fantastic! The Queen spent more time with you than with anybody else. You must've really said something to impress her. What was going on?" I didn't tell them the reason why. I just enjoyed the moment. I said, "Well, you know, we just got along."

The next day, I was hosting another big centennial show, this one at Lansdowne Park football stadium in Ottawa. Once again, at the end of the show all the performers lined up, with me at the very end. The Queen and Prince Philip worked their way down the line. He was not far behind her this time. And as she approached me, I was thinking, *Here comes my new best friend. I wonder what we'll talk about today?* I stood a little taller. My chest swelled up. I smiled. And when she got to me, she said, "Good show. Please tell me your name, and where you are from."

Me as Mark Twain.

Who Is . . .

MARK TWAIN?

In the early seventies, the new Global Network aired a TV show called *Witness to Yesterday*. Hosted by Patrick Watson, it was a one-on-one interview program in which actors—many of them famous or soon-to-be famous—appeared as key figures from world history. Sandy Dennis played Joan of Arc. Richard Dreyfuss played Billy the Kid. Jayne Meadows was Cleopatra. Christopher Plummer was the Duke of Wellington. Watson treated it seriously, as if they were real people, probing them about their interior lives as well as about their noteworthy actions.

One figure he wanted to interview was Mark Twain. And knowing my fascination with him, Patrick asked me if I would do the show.

I must admit I didn't read Twain much growing up. My interest in him didn't begin until seeing Hal Holbrook's work in *Mark Twain Tonight!* I soon read—and reread—a lot of his work. I own every book he wrote and several biographies of him. Over the years, people have even given me his autographs as gifts.

I agreed to Patrick's request to play Twain on *Witness to Yesterday*. They made a wig for me and some facial prosthetics. The difference between my performance and those other actors' was that theirs were scripted. Mine was entirely ad-libbed since I knew so many of Twain's lines by heart. Whatever Patrick wanted to ask, he was free to ask. And it went so well that instead of just doing one show, they stretched it into two.

Mark Twain is still my favorite philosopher. You have to look at philosophy as a way of life, and Twain's way of life was a very honest, straightforward one in which he respected humanity and cared about people—cared about their suffering. And he certainly was not partial to the oligarchs of the world. We need him today, actually. We could use him.

What Is . . .

COURAGE?

Of the thousands of letters, texts, and emails I've received since announcing my diagnosis, many of them have mentioned my courage. But that's not the way I look at courage. Courage is a conscious decision. You do it in a dangerous situation, when you have a choice. Here, there's no choice. I've been diagnosed with a disease that is probably going to kill me. And probably sooner than later. So courage does not enter into it.

That word—*courage*—is something I've thought about quite often in my life. If you're a guy, you worry about things like that. Well, maybe not all guys do. But I do. And there have only been, in my mind, a couple of times when I have demonstrated courage.

The one that stands out most occurred in my twenties in Canada. I had built a ski chalet up at Georgian Bay, about an hour drive from Sudbury. At that time, I was driving a 1965 Cadillac convertible, which I used as a pickup truck. I would haul ten-foot and twelve-foot lengths of lumber—one end on the dashboard, the other end sticking out through the unzipped rear window. Those cars were so long—both the '65 and the '66 Cadillac—that the lumber never extended past the rear bumper. Not too long ago I thought about buying one, just to revisit my youth, but it wouldn't fit in my garage, so I passed on it.

One Saturday night at my chalet there was a big pounding on the door. I went to the door and there was a young lady disheveled, in a terrible state, panicky as hell, saying, "He's going to kill me! He's going to kill me! He's overdosed on drugs, and he said he's going to kill me!"

I didn't know what she was talking about. It took me a couple of seconds to get her calmed down. She said her boyfriend in the chalet across the street had gone crazy and was after her to kill her. I told her, "Go sit down, call the police, and I'll go take a look."

I went across the street, and I arrived on the porch just as the front door opened. Out stepped this crazy-looking twenty-year-old with an ax in his hand. When he spotted me, he threatened me.

"Get out or I'll kill you," he said.

I don't know why, but as soon as he threatened to kill me, I put my hands in my pockets so I would not be perceived as a threat. Then I casually started talking to him. Like, "How you doing?" And within a few minutes he calmed down. We were talking for a while, until finally, in a moment of frustration, he just turned quickly, went back in the house, and slammed the door. I went back to my chalet, and the police arrived. They went across the street, and they took him into custody with no problem whatsoever.

So I've always thought of that as an example of courage in my life—especially the way I made a conscious, deliberate choice to put my hands in my pockets. That's what I remember most about that incident. Though I was probably just hiding my shaking hands.

Who Is . . .

ALAN THICKE?

After twelve years with the Canadian Broadcasting Corporation, I had a desire to spread my wings and look south of the border and see if there was something available in America. I had been in touch with Roone Arledge, head of ABC News and Sports, and he had expressed some interest in hiring me. I was waiting to schedule an audition with his office, but then one day—it was a Wednesday, I remember—I got a call from Alan Thicke.

Alan was also from Ontario and had been a popular game show and talk show host in Canada before moving to Los Angeles to work in American show business. I first met him at the start of his career when I was the host of an afternoon variety show called, logically enough, *After Noon*. It aired from 1:15 to 2:00 p.m., live at the Colonnade Theater in Toronto, in front of an audience. My cohost was Juliette, one of Canada's big singing stars. Our announcer was Bruce Marsh, Canada's top commercial announcer. The format was similar to a late-night talk show. We had a band that played music. I'd come out and do a monologue, then interview guests. Alan was part of a singing duo that appeared on the show.

"I'm writing a new game show for NBC," he said over the phone. The show was called *The Wizard of Odds*. It was to be filmed in the round, so there was no place for cue cards. They needed a host with experience who could think on his feet, and they were looking for a new face.

"We've kind of exhausted our list of potential hosts here in the U.S.," Alan said. "Would you be interested?"

"Sure."

"Okay. I'm going to come up to Toronto and we'll talk."

He didn't waste any time. He flew in the next day. He picked me up in a car and drove us to his parents' house outside of Toronto. There he explained the game to me, and we did some run-throughs. Then Friday we did more rehearsal games with members of his family—his brother, his sister, his mom and dad. And then Saturday morning we flew to New York.

I went to the Hilton hotel and met with Marty Pasetta, who was going to be the director. He had me rehearse all day. At six o'clock we had some contestants come into our rehearsal hall— they pulled them off the street in front of the Hilton—and we ran the game. We were cruising along beautifully. We had a really good game going. Then we got to the bonus round. I had rehearsed the bonus round for about two hours. There were three doors, with a prize behind each. If you picked door #1 and it didn't contain a big *X*, you could then select from door #2 or #3. The idea was that hopefully you could pick two doors that had prizes and avoid the one that didn't.

Unfortunately, the contestant who was in the bonus round picked the *X* door first. So I said, "Well, there goes two hours of rehearsal. It's over. The game is over. Thank you very much. Goodbye!"

This was about six thirty. I went to my room, got my bags, and went directly to LaGuardia Airport. I took a plane back to Toronto and got home in time to watch the second period of a hockey game, which made me feel good. Around eleven o'clock that night I got a phone call from Alan.

"We'd like you to come to Los Angeles to do a pilot," he said.

"When?" I asked.

He gave me the dates.

"Okay," I said. "I'll free up some time," which was not going to be a problem.

I had accumulated twelve or thirteen weeks of annual leave, so I was sitting pretty. I was one of the few bachelors on the announcer staff at the CBC, and whenever we had statutory holidays and I was scheduled to be off, I knew that some of the married guys would like to have time to spend with their families. So I would volunteer. I would go to our scheduling guy and say, "Look, why don't you talk to so-and-so, and if he wants the day off I'll take his shift."

I flew to Los Angeles and did the pilot. And before the day was out they said, "You got the job."

They were going to start taping the series immediately. I thought, *I have twelve weeks of leave coming. I'm not going to resign from the CBC because we're just being picked up for thirteen weeks. We'll see how it goes.*

Only after we were picked up for the second thirteen weeks did I resign. I put my house up for sale and moved all my furniture to LA. It was a bitch getting into the country with the work permits. Immigration was rough even back then. U.S. unions didn't want any more Canadians coming in and stealing jobs from Americans.

I managed to get my green card application approved because my new employer said I had a specific skill that no other American hosts had, which was being able to work in the round without cue cards. My employers also said I had a photographic memory, which was a lie.

The Answer Is . . .

LOS ANGELES

I wasn't sad about leaving Canada. It helped that my sister, Barbara, lived in Los Angeles. She had moved there a few years earlier to be with her boyfriend. I'd visited her, and I liked the city. Once I moved here, I got to know it well. I joke that back then it was a much kinder, gentler place. You would drive up to a four-way stop and there'd be a car with the right-of-way, but the driver would smile and wave you through the intersection. Nowadays the guy will still wave you through but he doesn't use all the fingers on his hand. I once told that joke to one of our audiences, and somebody piped up, "Maybe he recognized you."

But back then it really did feel like a small town. I remember waiting in line at a Brown Derby restaurant, and the actor Gordon MacRae, who'd starred in the film versions of *Oklahoma!* and *Carousel*, was standing just behind me. I heard him comment to his companion, "Things have really changed. In the old days they wouldn't have had me stand in line like this."

I was in hog heaven. I was where things happened. The center of the entertainment industry. Not making a whole lot of money but enough to survive comfortably in a new apartment. I was having a great time.

In front of *The Wizard of Odds* wheel. What can I
say about that suit except it was the seventies?

I made friends with the executive producer of *The Wizard of Odds*, Burt Sugarman, who also created and produced the rock-and-roll variety show *The Midnight Special*. Burt taught me how to play backgammon and then discovered he could never beat me at backgammon. Which ticked him off. He introduced me to a whole new society of friends and show business personalities. Because I was a bachelor and the new kid in town, I'd get invited to a lot of dinner parties and would meet more of the celebrities whose work I admired.

Richard Gully, the former publicity head for Jack Warner, took a liking to me, and he would invite me to dinner parties at the Bistro in Beverly Hills. I got to know actress Polly Bergen, who at the time was married to Creative Management Associates cofounder Freddie Fields. They introduced me to some of their friends.

Later, when I became the host of the game show *High Rollers*, I worked with and became friends with two wonderful women, Ruta Lee and Elaine Stewart. The show was a simplified version of craps that used two oversized dice. Ruta and Elaine would roll the dice for the contestants. Though never a major star, Ruta knew *everybody*. She had friends in all areas of show business and was always eager to introduce me to them. One time, she asked me to help her organize a ball for a charity she worked with and invited me to sit at the head table with her and all her famous friends. Elaine was married to Merrill Heatter, who along with Bob Quigley was the co-producer of *High Rollers* and cocreator of *The Hollywood Squares*. Elaine and Merrill introduced me to yet another group of celebrities. For instance, Heatter-Quigley always hosted an annual party at some out-of-town destination. One year, they took everybody to

Jamaica. In addition to myself, Ruta, and Elaine, there were a lot of the stars who'd been on *The Hollywood Squares*, such as Vincent Price, Jonathan Winters, and George Gobel. Art Fleming, who was hosting *Jeopardy!* at the time, was also a guest. He was just as he appeared on TV, a true gentleman. All of a sudden I was surrounded by these people I'd enjoyed watching for years. I mean, *The Hollywood Squares* was the highlight of daytime television for me. And now I was one of them.

I'll never forget how openhearted and generous all these strangers were to a green thirty-three-year-old from Canada who had never experienced this kind of attention or operated in this kind of milieu. Whether it was this kind group or Father Danis and Big John L'abbé, I have always been fortunate to have people take me under their wing.

My *High Rollers* colleagues and good friends
Ruta Lee (*left*) and Elaine Stewart (*right*).

Your bones may be in jeopardy.

One in five osteoporosis victims is male. Luckily, fat free milk has the calcium bones need to help beat it. Beating your Harvard Ph.D. opponents? Well, that's another story.

got milk?

Participating in the famous ad campaign for milk
in the nineties. I really do love the stuff.

The Answer Is . . .

CURSING

I mentioned in the introduction to this book that I would later explain my penchant for cursing. It was a deliberate action on my part. Around this time in my career, I had the world by the tail. I was the talented newcomer in broadcasting. I was the bright, fair-haired boy. I was good at my job. I didn't drink, didn't smoke, didn't do drugs. There were no big negatives associated with me.

And that caused problems, because it held me back from becoming one of the guys, if you will—one of the group. People can be suspicious of someone who's so chaste. They're afraid to let their guard down and be themselves for fear they'll be judged. I needed a vice. I remembered my childhood friend Maurice from back in Sudbury, and so I decided to add more salt to my language. I started cursing, or to be more precise, injecting curse words into my conversations. But it didn't help me become one of the guys. It just made me look like a jerk. My bad.

In recent years I have gotten away from it a little, replacing it with something I consider to be even better: booze. Or, at least, the suggestion of booze. What I've discovered in my conversations with studio audiences who come to the tapings is that no matter what question they ask, if I provide the same answer I'll always get a laugh.

"You look pretty fit. What do you do to stay in shape?"

"I drink."

"How do you prepare for the show?"

"I drink."

"What do you do when you're not working?"

"I drink."

So that has been a suitable replacement for cursing. I don't really drink that much. Having seen the way my father drank, it never interested me. Occasionally I'll have a glass of chardonnay, but my drink of choice is low-fat milk. Quite often I'll get up in the middle of the night, go to the refrigerator, and get a full glass of 1 percent milk. It's become a habit. I drink low-fat milk and chardonnay—but not together.

What Are . . .

HASH BROWNIES?

I did have one unintentional experience with drugs. Not long after I arrived in Los Angeles, I was invited to a dinner party in Malibu. There were chocolate brownies on a plate in the living room. Well, I love chocolate. The hosts said, "Go ahead, help yourself." I had four or five of them. I did not realize they were hash brownies. Mr. Naive here. The party was on a Friday night. The drugs knocked me out so much I spent the weekend laid out in their guest bedroom and didn't leave their home until Monday morning. Talk about embarrassment.

I may have looked like a hippie, but I wasn't cut out for the lifestyle.

The Category Is . . .

LUXURY AUTOMOBILES

When I was a child, I was fascinated by cars. I would cut advertisements out of newspapers and magazines and paste them into a big scrapbook. It was easier to have a scrapbook of cars in those days because there were only three major American producers, plus the Austin Motor Company in England. I'd keep track of the models, the new engines, and all that stuff.

During my teenage years, I drove my dad's Ford. Through much of my twenties, I drove my enormous '65 Cadillac convertible. When I got to LA, I drove a secondhand car for a bit. But then in 1973 I made my first big purchase.

Burt Sugarman had a collection of Rolls-Royces. One of his good friends, who was a dealer in Rolls-Royces and Bentleys, approached me one day and said, "I've got this great convertible here for you. It's a left-hand drive," and they didn't make too many of those. It was a 1956 Bentley Mulliner Park Ward Convertible. That car was a beauty. I bought it for $34,000—and that was $34,000 in *1973*.

One day I was driving the convertible home from the NBC studios in Burbank. I was on the Ventura Freeway and all of a sudden a new white Rolls-Royce convertible pulls up beside me. The driver was Wilt Chamberlain. Sitting next to him was this beautiful blond woman.

He leaned out his window and said, "Fine-looking car."

I looked at him, and I said, "Fine-looking companion." And I drove off.

I used to take a particular delight in parking the car near Johnny Carson's spot on the NBC lot. He filmed his show in Stage 1, and we filmed ours in Stage 3. He had his reserved spot outside. Most days he was driving a Corvette. I would park as close as possible. I knew he would take a look at my Bentley.

After the divorce from my first wife, Elaine, I needed money for a house. So I sold the Bentley for $54,000. If I wanted to buy it back today it would cost me a million and a half.

I also bought a white 1956 Jaguar XK140 Roadster and a red 1971 Italia Spyder. There's an interesting story behind the Spyder. Back when I was in Canada in the late sixties, I had seen a commercial in which they used a Ferrari Daytona convertible.

I said, "Oh my God, what a lovely car." I called the Ferrari dealership and found out the car sold for $26,000. I said, "Oh God, I can't afford $26,000 for a car."

Then I discovered the Italia, which had a similar design. So I found a used one in California, and I fixed it up. I renovated the interior. I wanted to reupholster the seats and went around looking for leather. I found one leather shop that was having a sale on very nice brown mottled leather that had been used to redo all the superior court judges' seats in the county of Los Angeles. This shop had the leftovers. "Hey, I'll take that." I had an upholstery guy do the seats, because there was a lot of stitching involved. But I did the doors and the floors myself.

That was a wonderful car, but unfortunately, here in Southern California with a lot of stop-and-go traffic and the tremendous heat, it would constantly overheat—even though I put in a radiator and two extra fans. I would only drive it occasionally. It got to be a coffee table. It just sat there in the garage. So I finally decided, *I'm going to sell this one*. And I sold it to a guy who drove it to Arizona.

I told him about the overheating. I said, "You have to be careful."

Well, he left California about eleven in the morning and drove straight to Arizona. He called me that night and said, "Made it all the way. Not a problem."

Only about five hundred Spyders were ever made. I originally bought it for $6,000. I sold it to that guy for $30,000. I saw a couple of years ago that Sotheby's auctioned it off for $179,200. They even used my name in the catalog copy. "Finished in a striking shade of dark metallic red, this Italia Spyder once belonged to the famed *Jeopardy!* host, Alex Trebek."

I am no longer into fancy cars. I am past the age when I need to have a car to impress people. These days I drive a Dodge Ram 1500 truck with a Hemi. It's practical, because I do so much work around the house, repairs and stuff, and I'm always hauling tools and things. But don't get me wrong . . . driving a truck doesn't make me a redneck. I don't have a gun rack in it. I have a wine rack.

Reunited with my old Jag in 2019.

The photo RM Sotheby's used to auction off the Italia Spyder I once owned.

A proud truck owner.

With my first wife, Elaine, and Nicky.

The Answer Is . . .

FAMILY

Shortly after a friend of mine got divorced, he was set up on a date. He went to pick this lady up. She was also recently divorced. He walked into her home and noticed there was a grand piano.

"Oh, what a beautiful grand piano," he said. "Do you play?"

"No," she said. "My husband does. It was his piano. And I insisted that I get it in the divorce."

"I see," my friend said. "Good night."

He walked out and left her there. He did not go through with the date because he thought it was terrible she would do that out of spite. I have never experienced anything like that with my first wife, Elaine.

I met Elaine in Toronto. She hosted a couple of television programs, including a daily talk show that was groundbreaking for how frankly it addressed sexual topics. She had been married before and had a daughter named Nicky. She was around six when Elaine and I got together, and cute as all get out. The two of them moved to Los Angeles not long after I got settled in, and Elaine and I were married in 1974.

We bought a house up on Mulholland Drive, and Elaine invited my mother, who was living in Florida, to come to California and live with us and help raise Nicky. There was a guesthouse on the property. It was Elaine's idea, not mine, to have Mom come. And it worked out great. Elaine got involved with a lot of charitable work with a group of Beverly Hills ladies, I was taping *High Rollers*, and Mom would look after Nicky. It was a marvelous arrangement.

We divorced in 1981. It was amicable. We didn't use attorneys. I think it cost about $320 in fees. We sold the house, and Elaine got the cash. I got a mortgage. She went out and bought another house. My mother went to live with her and continued to raise Nicky. I had no cash, so I borrowed a little money from Elaine and bought a house . . . directly across the street from her.

I know it sounds unconventional, but it suited all of us. My mother would look after Nicky at Elaine's house and then come over to help me take care of my place.

My relationships with Elaine and Nicky remain strong. Though I never adopted Nicky—her biological father was alive at the time—I refer to her as my daughter by osmosis. Elaine and my current wife, Jean, are close. When my kids, Emily and Matthew, were in high school, Elaine would give them summer jobs. Of all Hollywood-type wedding-divorce scenarios you can think of, ours is probably the least confrontational and contentious. There were never any problems whatsoever that made us curse each other. We have get-togethers every year, usually at our house, but this year Nicky hosted Christmas dinner at her place. Elaine and her husband, Peter, were there, and Jeanie and me, and Nicky and Emily and Matthew, who flew in from New York. We're all a very close-knit, happy family.

Dancing with Nicky at my and
Jean's wedding, 1990.

The extended Trebek clan at holiday dinner, 2019.

Clockwise from top left: At work on *The $128,000 Question, Battlestars,* and *Double Dare.*

What Is . . .

THE TEN-THOUSAND-HOUR RULE?

My career during those early years in Los Angeles was a bit erratic and unusual. I was being offered hosting jobs for all kinds of shows. After just one year, *The Wizard of Odds* was canceled. It was canceled on a Friday and replaced on Monday by *High Rollers*, also hosted by me. That doesn't happen very often. *High Rollers* was an easier game to host than *The Wizard of Odds* had been.

The Wizard of Odds required a lot of mathematical skills. Because of the Compliance and Practices Department, if I said, "There is one chance in 6.27 that this will happen," and it was actually one in 6.28, they would come back and correct me.

I remember one show we got to the bonus round, where there were ten items each associated with a number. For instance, if I said "the Stooges," that number was three. If I said "number of weeks in a year," that number was fifty-two. It was the job of the contestant to combine four of those items and keep the total below a certain number. And if they did that, they won a car. In this particular bonus round, the contestant just missed coming in below the number.

"That's too bad," I said. "If you had chosen this other item . . ." Then I took another look at the numbers. "Wait a minute, the math doesn't work. We screwed up. We made a mistake. You shouldn't be punished for our mistake. So I'm going to give you the car anyway."

The audience went crazy. After the show, I was walking to my dressing room, feeling good about myself for my wisdom and fairness. Burt Sugarman saw me and stopped me.

"Alex," he said, "next time when you notice we've screwed up, we'll just stop tape and rectify it. Don't give the car away."

At *High Rollers* there was a lot less pressure on me. It was just rolling dice. *High Rollers* lasted two years. While I was doing that, I was also hosting *The $128,000 Question*, which filmed in Toronto. So I had to fly back and forth to tape both shows. Then *High Rollers* was off for half a year.

During that time, I hosted *Battlestars*. I've always referred to that show as "the son of *Hollywood Squares*." *Hollywood Squares* had nine celebrities. *Battlestars* had a smaller budget, so we could only afford six. *Hollywood Squares* had squares. *Battlestars* had triangles. The performer who came out of *Battlestars* and enjoyed the greatest success later on was Jerry Seinfeld. My favorite memory of that show was from another of our celebrity panelists, Tom Poston. Tom was a veteran film and TV actor who at that time was best known for his work on the sitcom *Mork & Mindy*. I was interviewing one of the contestants, a young lady who had just relocated to Los Angeles.

"Why did you come to California?" I asked.

"I came to find a husband," she said.

Without missing a beat, Tom shouted out, "Whose husband did you come to find?"

Battlestars didn't last more than six months. I was then offered a job to host a game show called *Pitfall*, to be taped in Vancouver.

This was during a difficult time in my life. My father was sick with cancer, and Elaine and I had just divorced. I needed the money for my new house. The job was supposed to pay me $49,000, which was a nice amount of dough back then. The one caveat was that I had to be a member of the Canadian union, otherwise they couldn't hire me. No problem. I'd long been a member of the Alliance of Canadian Cinema, Television and Radio Artists. So I signed the contract. Then I got up there, and the union said I couldn't work on the show because the production company was not a signatory to the union agreement. There was a big dispute. The head of the show said that if I didn't perform, they were going to sue me for breach of contract. And the union said if I did perform, I'd be in big trouble with them.

Finally, they got it all resolved. We did thirteen weeks of the show, and they paid me. Then we did another thirteen weeks, but this time the check didn't clear. I went to the union and asked them to help. They said there was nothing they could do. That really ticked me off. I had stood up for them during the dispute with the production company, and now they weren't willing to stand up for me. Through other channels, I discovered that I was one of dozens of people the show hadn't paid, such as the set carpenters and other craftspeople.

I framed the check and hung it on the wall behind my desk where I'm writing this. It was the only time in my life I ever got stiffed on a payment. Whenever I think of the guy who did it, I recall Mark Twain's famous line: "If ever I should hear of his sudden demise I will forgo all other forms of entertainment in order to attend his funeral."

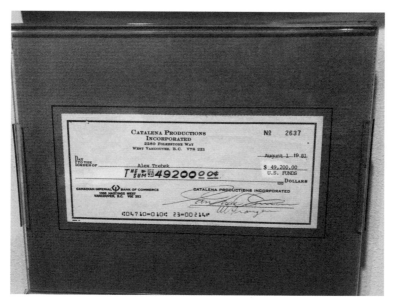

My memento from *Pitfall*.

I then hosted a show called *Double Dare*, which gave me my first opportunity to work with the legendary producer Mark Goodson. From Mark, I learned it doesn't matter who comes up with a good idea. When I worked at the CBC, I would make suggestions to producers, and they weren't always well-received. There was one producer-director who was a real jerk. I had been hosting this sports program for a couple of years. It was a show that filled time after football games on Sundays. We never knew how long the show would be. It depended on what time the game ended. If the game ended at 3:20 and we were supposed to be off the air at four, then we had forty minutes to fill. If the game ended at 3:50, then we had only ten minutes to fill. To deal with this, we set up a rack of sports highlight reels of various lengths, and while I ad-libbed an intro, a technician would cue up the reel whose timing most closely worked with our requirements. Well, this new producer-director came in and put all the different-length film clips on one big reel. So if we needed to fill only a couple minutes it wouldn't work.

"I don't think that's a good idea," I started to tell him. He cut me off.

"Are you the producer-director of this show?" he asked.

"No," I said.

"What's your job?" he asked.

"I'm the host," I said.

"Then I'll handle it," he said.

And of course the arrogant SOB screwed it up.

Then I met Mark Goodson. When we first started working on *Double Dare*, I made a suggestion to him.

"That's a good idea," he said. *Wow*, I thought, *Los Angeles is a different world than Canada.*

Whatever my good idea was, it wasn't good enough to keep *Double Dare* on the air. That show lasted twenty-six weeks at most. Then *High Rollers* came back for two and a half years.

In the midst of all this, I went back to Canada once more to film a show called *Stars on Ice* for the private network CTV. I was not a figure skater, but I had played hockey. They put me in skates, and I'd get out there every week with the entertainers. They had set up this large skating rink in one of the stages. The producer, Mike Steele, had directed shows in the United States, and he understood the concept of show business in a way that most Canadian TV executives did not. CTV's lighter schedule put a great deal of pressure on the CBC to loosen up a bit and change its way of doing things. He wanted viewers to see TV not just as a government entity providing educational programming and prestigious dramas, but also shows that could make people laugh. Sure, the CBC had broadcast some great comedians such as Wayne and Shuster, who I grew up listening to on the radio and whose early television specials I loved. But for the most part, the CBC was more serious and straitlaced until CTV came along with programs like *Stars on Ice*.

In case you've lost count by now, that's seven jobs in ten years. I never felt frustrated by the lack of continuity during those years. That's just the business. For all the shows that are hits, there are dozens more that aren't. I was just happy to have a job. There's a lot to be said for being gainfully employed in the entertainment industry.

The producer Bob Noah, who I worked with on *High Rollers*,

once said to me, "Alex, never turn down a job. You never know if another offer is going to come along."

For a long time, as long as I was able to, I did not turn down jobs.

And I never doubted my talent either. I never took it personally when a show got canceled. I knew I was good. Because I had experience. I had spent more than a decade at the CBC. The author Malcolm Gladwell—also Canadian, I might add—has famously written about the "ten-thousand-hour rule." He said that in order to master a craft, you have to spend at least ten thousand hours doing it. That's what my time at the CBC was. Hosting every kind of program imaginable—it was a perfect apprenticeship.

Recently, I saw a pilot for one of those early game shows, and I said, "Damn, I was *good*." I don't always view myself the same way now. I don't always come away saying, "Oh, you did a good job." But I look at the nuances I brought to that pilot, and I say, "Man, that was fast. That was sharp. You were on your game. You were good."

That was no fluke. I had put in my ten thousand hours. And I continued to improve and gain experience with those early game shows. So when I got invited to host yet another show, this one called *Jeopardy!*, I was ready.

The Answer Is . . .

LUCK

Gladwell's thesis is that everyone considered a master in their field has most likely logged ten thousand hours. However, just because you've put in your ten thousand hours doesn't guarantee you will ever be *considered*. It doesn't guarantee that your talent will be seen and acknowledged by others. Those ten thousand hours don't guarantee you an opportunity. That has a lot to do with timing.

"Hey, I'm the best train conductor in the world."

"Yes, but people are traveling by plane now."

My broadcasting experience wouldn't have mattered much if they hadn't been producing game shows at the time—if Westerns or reality television or *Judge Judy*-type courtroom shows had been in vogue.

Yes, hard work and experience are essential. But so is timing. And luck. Don't ever discount the importance of luck in terms of determining your opportunities and your future.

One day, I got a phone call from Bob Murphy, Merv Griffin's vice president.

"We need your help," he said.

I was hosting *Battlestars* at the time. Chuck Woolery was hosting another NBC game show, *Wheel of Fortune*, which Merv had created in the mid-seventies.

"We're scheduled to tape a *Wheel* tournament this weekend," Bob said, "and Chuck is in the hospital. We need somebody to step in at the last minute. And we thought you were the one host who could do that and wouldn't need a lot of prep."

"Sure," I said. "I'll help out."

"Just one thing," Bob said. "You can't mention his circumstances."

"Fine," I said. So that's what I did. I hosted the tournament.

Not long after, Chuck left *Wheel* for good. I'm not sure what happened. One story is that Chuck tried to put pressure on Merv for more money. Merv was notably stingy with performers. He did not like paying the going rate for his hosts or on-camera people. So he let Chuck go. Another story was that Chuck quit. Whatever occurred, Merv hired Pat Sajak to replace him. How did that work out? Merv always had a great eye for talent.

After a couple of years with Pat hosting, *Wheel* went into syndication. But it was only airing on a small number of stations, because it was a half-hour show and in those days syndication was an hour block before prime time. In order to expand *Wheel* to more stations, they needed another half hour to go with it. So someone suggested, "Why don't we bring *Jeopardy!* back on the air and make it part of a one-hour block with *Wheel?*"

Merv and Bob remembered the favor I did for them filling in for Chuck. They called me up.

"We're going to bring *Jeopardy!* into syndication," they said. "We think if we package it with *Wheel* we'll have a good thing here. And we'd like you to host it."

At least, that's the way Merv and Bob would remember it. They always claimed it was their idea to ask me to host *Jeopardy!* This was disputed by Roger King, co-owner of King World Productions, which had bought the syndication rights to the show and distributed it. He claimed hiring me was his idea—well, actually, his mother's idea. Roger said his mother had told him, "If you ever do a quiz show, you've gotta get this guy Alex Trebek to host."

Whoever's idea it was, I got lucky.

The Answer Is . . .

INGENUITY

Before I got off that phone call with Merv and Bob, I jokingly asked a very important question:

"Will you pay me?"

"Yes," they said.

"Okay," I said. "I'm your man."

Then I found out *what* they were going to pay me. Like I said, Merv was stingy. So I asked if I could produce the show as well and receive extra payment as the producer, and they agreed. Even then, I made less than I had made in previous shows I'd only hosted.

In addition to hosting, I produced *Jeopardy!* for the first three years. I made one significant change after the first season, which we've kept up all these years. That first season, contestants could ring in immediately when they saw the clue. It caused a lot of confusion among viewers at home. They would be watching and they'd see a contestant's light come on, but I would call on another contestant because their light had come on first and had gone off before the camera turned from the clue to the contestants. It drove the audience nuts. So I changed that. Now, a contestant cannot ring in until after I've read the clue in its entirety. An unintended benefit was that it gave viewers a better experience of playing along. A lot

September 10, 1984: the first time viewers saw me
walk out to Johnny Gilbert's introduction.

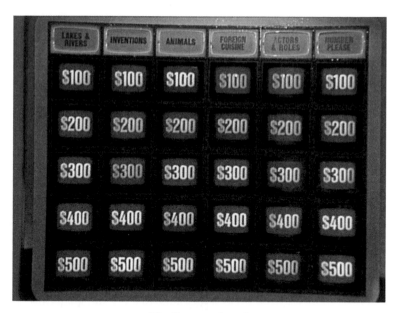

The first gameboard.

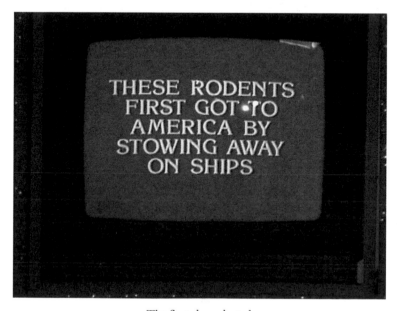

The first clue selected.

of people play at home with ballpoint pens or something similar as buzzers, and that change made it easier for them to read ahead and beat the on-air contestants. I'm often asked what's the secret to ringing in first. It's simple: Know as much as you can about the categories and clues. The more you know, the faster your thumb is.

We had a very tight budget during those seasons I produced. This was before computers. The writers typed their questions on three-by-five index cards on IBM Selectrics. For a few years, the category cards at the top of the gameboard were printed. Someone would have to change them between rounds. It wasn't as antiquated as when Art Fleming hosted the show in the sixties, and you'd sometimes see a hand coming into the camera frame and pulling the cards. But it was close. For our gameboard, I finally found an affordable used chyron machine from CBS Television, and we started using that to run it. So I had to use a lot of ingenuity. I enjoyed it for the same reason I enjoy fixing things around the house. I'm a problem solver.

Through the ensuing years, under new producers, especially Harry Friedman, who has just left the show after twenty years at the helm, *Jeopardy!* has made a conscious effort to stay ahead of the curve. We were the first game or quiz show to broadcast in high definition. With the hiring of the Clue Crew, we introduced a whole new way of presenting clues from locations all around the world. We started tournaments honoring teachers and students. Stars from the entertainment and political worlds, including two presidents, made appearances on the show, all in an attempt for us to stay fresh and relevant with the times.

But in the early years, putting the show together wasn't the only

Handwriting on a computer screen was an innovative idea, but it took some time for the technology to catch up. (Those answers are supposed to read "What Is Texas?" and "What Is Martin Luther King Jr. Day?")

challenge. We also struggled getting people to watch. Even though *Jeopardy!* was supposed to be packaged with *Wheel*, it wasn't always. For example, initially *Wheel* was on at 7:00 p.m. in Los Angeles and *Jeopardy!* wouldn't come on until midnight.

King World, the show's distributor, was very concerned. Michael King came to me after we'd been on the air for three or four weeks.

"The show's too tough," he said. "The material is too difficult. The audience can't relate to it. That's why the ratings are not taking off."

"You sure?" I asked.

"Yeah, yeah," he said. "You gotta trust me."

"All right," I said. "I'll soften up all the material."

Now keep in mind, we had already taped two months of programming. The next time I saw Michael, I said, "Did you notice that the material got a lot easier?"

"Yeah!" he said. "Thank you so much for doing that. It's playing a lot better now."

I hadn't done a damn thing. The shows were already taped. They were in the bag. I just lied to him.

What Is . . .

"A TIME FOR TONY"?

Back in those early days of *Jeopardy!*, when I was both hosting and producing the show, I used to answer all the mail. I'd send a response to everything, the fan letters as well as the hate mail. One day, Merv Griffin saw me doing this and said, "You know how I handle the nasty mail?" He grabbed a letter, balled it up, and threw it into the wastebasket.

I still take the input we receive from viewers very seriously—some might even say too seriously. If someone writes to criticize either me or the show, I probably spend way too much time and energy pondering their complaints and worrying about my performance. While I am no longer able to respond to *every* letter or email or comment on social media, I still try to answer as many as I can.

Merv was actually a very warm man. He had the unique ability to draw you in and make you feel like whatever you were saying was the only thing that mattered to him in that moment. He was not laid-back. He wasn't cool. He was excited and engaged. That's why he was such a great talk show host. He especially loved storytellers. That's why he frequently had the two Orsons on his show—Orson Bean and Orson Welles. They knew how to tell great stories. It's a

With Merv Griffin.

lost art these days, when we only seem to have the attention span for sound bites.

The few times I spent with Merv were very special, but we didn't have much of a relationship. He left *Jeopardy!* alone completely. He involved himself the first year or two in the design and colors of the set. And he did guest star with me on an episode of *The Golden Girls* that was shot on our set. But that was it. He never got involved in the material. His ex-wife, Julann, had originally come up with the idea for the show. As the story goes, shortly after the quiz show scandals of the 1950s, Merv was trying to come up with an idea for a new game show. Julann suggested giving the contestants the answers.

"That's what put people in jail!" Merv said.

Julann then gave him an example of how it would work. I have heard two different stories about what she suggested as the first *Jeopardy!* clue. One version has her saying, "The answer is 5,280," and Merv asking, "How many feet are in a mile?" The other version has her saying, "79 Wistful Vista," and him asking, "Where did Fibber McGee and Molly live?" Whichever one it was, it convinced Merv to pursue the idea. And that's how *Jeopardy!* came to be.

But his show, his baby, was *Wheel of Fortune*. He took a great deal of pleasure—and was good at it—in coming up with the word puzzles for *Wheel*. But he had no interest whatsoever in *Jeopardy!* That was Bob Murphy's bailiwick.

Merv and Bob had been best friends as kids growing up in Northern California. Bob became successful in the real estate business, and Merv asked him to join his company. Bob eventually became president of Merv Griffin Entertainment.

Bob and I got to be best friends over the years. He's Matthew's godfather. In the early days of *Jeopardy!*, people would constantly challenge us to trivia games. There was a party one night hosted by the King brothers in which they decided they wanted to challenge Bob and me. Eight people got together on one team against the two of us. And we beat 'em. We beat 'em badly. I maintain we won because we made the perfect team. We complemented each other. Bob knew all that could be known, and I knew all the rest.

One fact about Merv that some people don't know: he wrote the *Jeopardy!* theme song. It's called "Think!"—though Merv originally wrote it as a lullaby for his son entitled "A Time for Tony." Every time that song airs, Merv—and, since his death in 2007, his estate—gets a royalty. Even when, say, Paul Shaffer would play it when I made an entrance as a guest on David Letterman's show, Merv would get a check. Shortly before he died, Merv admitted that the little *Jeopardy!* think music had earned him close to $80 million—more than $3 million a year for twenty-four years, plus little extras here and there when it's used outside of the show.

People ask me, "Do you ever get tired of hearing it?" No, it's just part of the show. I'm used to it. Granted, I don't go around humming it. But I enjoy it when it's played at a baseball game when a manager goes to the mound to make a pitching change, or when the referees at an NFL game are going to the video replay. It's part of Americana. It's something people recognize immediately. Same thing if somebody says, "Hey, you didn't phrase that in the form of a question." Everybody in the room knows exactly what the reference is.

The Answer Is . . .

ANOTHER LESSON
IN HUMILITY

In the early years of *Jeopardy!*, in order to help grow the show's audience I did PR trips around the country. Pat Sajak, Vanna White, and I would go out on the road together because we were pitching *Wheel* and *Jeopardy!* as a package deal. Mostly we'd visit local morning shows. I didn't mind it. I'm gregarious enough that I could roll with the punches with the local anchors. I remember going on Oprah's show in Chicago back when it was on in the morning. (Before long, King World would sign her to a syndication deal too.) One time, the three of us were guests on Sally Jesse Raphael's show in St. Louis. She asked us who our showbiz heroes were. Pat said somebody like Walter Cronkite.

"What about you, Alex?" Sally asked.

"Arnold Stang," I said. Stang was a comic actor who was popular in the forties and fifties. The audience was totally clueless and utterly silent. But Pat laughed. He was probably the only one in the room who knew who Arnold Stang was. Now, take a break from this book and go look him up.

Another thing I did to help build the show's popularity was go on the road for our very first contestant searches. We still do them to this day. The contestant department travels from city to city. They bring a group of hopefuls into a conference room and give them a fifty-question test. Then they pick up those tests and go grade them. During that time, the applicants don't have much to do but wait. So in those early years, I would occasionally come along and surprise the groups and take questions.

One time in New York, I did that. A few minutes into the question-and-answer period, a guy at the back of the room raised his hand.

"Yes, sir?" I asked.

"Who are you?" he said.

"I beg your pardon?"

"Who are you?" he asked.

All of the people around him kind of gave him a strange look.

"I don't understand," I said.

"Well," he explained, "I was just walking by outside the hotel, and I saw this sign that said '*Jeopardy!* Testing.' So I thought I'd come in. I have never heard of the show, and I don't know who you are." Then he started apologizing.

"Don't apologize," I told him. "You don't have to apologize. There are a lot of people out there who don't watch television. And I don't take it personally that they are not familiar with the show. I hope that they will look in and discover us, but it's okay. You don't have to say, 'I'm sorry' for not knowing who I am."

It was another lesson in humility, just in case I hadn't been sufficiently humbled by my encounter all those years before with Her Majesty the Queen. I still don't know if the guy passed the test.

The Answer Is . . .

GIVING BACK

Around 1984, the Ethiopian famine was in the news, and they were showing all those terrible photos and film clips on television about the suffering that was going on. A friend of mine, the actress Carol Lawrence, was doing some public-service announcements about the crisis for the humanitarian organization World Vision. I called her up and said, "Is there anything I can do to help, Carol? Don't hesitate to ask or tell them about me."

Within a couple of weeks I got a phone call from World Vision. They said, "We got your message and would like you to join us and help out."

They started sending me all over the world. In the more than thirty years I've been involved with the organization, I've made more than a dozen international trips—most of them to Africa. I've been to Ethiopia, Ghana, Nigeria, Uganda, Kenya, Tanzania, Mozambique, and South Africa. When I first went to Africa, I immediately felt at a visceral level, *This is home. This is where I come from. I belong here.* I feel that every time I go there. I know that's where civilization began, and I feel it in my gut. You don't have to tell me. There's just something about it. I stand in Africa and I say, "I'm home."

In Ethiopia, a mother asks me to take her child.

Once in Ethiopia, I was helping distribute food and blankets and pots and pans to families who had registered to receive help from World Vision. There was one woman who had not registered. She wasn't on the list. She was in tears and gave me her baby.

"Take my baby," she said. "You look after my baby." She meant permanently. She was worried she wouldn't be able to keep her baby alive.

There have been a lot of experiences like that with World Vision. I was in Thailand visiting an orphanage run by a priest and some nuns. There were two sections. There was an indoor section with a lot of cots where the babies were pretty sick. And there was a large outdoor playpen for toddlers who were relatively healthy. While the sister-nurse was taking me around explaining what was going on, one of the toddlers—this nude little boy—came up to my side and raised his arms. I picked him up, and I carried him around while I took the tour. At the end of the tour, I went to put him down and he started to cry. I tried to calm him down, but he was inconsolable.

"What's wrong?" I asked the sister-nurse. "What did I do?"

"You didn't do anything," she said. "They have so little physical contact with human beings that once you pick them up they don't want to let go. They feel so loved and warm. They don't want to lose that."

When I heard that, I started to cry myself.

In Mozambique, I ran into another little boy. He was wearing a loincloth. He had a hoop made of wire, about the size of a bicycle wheel, and a stick with a little crook in it. He would work his wheel with the stick, and just push it along. That was his toy.

In Ethiopia for World Vision. I was much younger then, and could even manage to smile while helping distribute sixty-pound bags of grain.

In Bangladesh, there was a mother of two. There was never a husband around. She was seated working in a cardboard box that was four-by-four feet. She had a two-year-old next to her and a younger infant on her chest. Her job was to smash boulders the size of a cantaloupe and break them down into much smaller pieces. Then they would use that as gravel on the road.

I thought, *My God, she's smashing these rocks and that two-year-old is sitting nearby. A small piece of stone could fly and hit that kid in the eye.*

She had one pan and one sari. That was it. That's all she owned.

When you go through experiences like these over the years and you see man's inhumanity to man and how much suffering is out there, it affects you. You can't stand by passively and just say, "Well, it's not going to bother me. I'm okay. I'm going back to LA." You want to do something. You want to help. So I continued to help World Vision, both financially and with my time.

Then one day my accountant came to me, and he asked, "Do you like the way the government is spending your tax money?"

"No," I said.

"Would you like to have more say in it?" he asked.

"Sure," I said.

"Well, why don't you and Jean form a charitable foundation," he said, "and that way you can decide where your monies are spent."

So we did. It just changed my philosophy completely. Now instead of giving small amounts to a hundred different charities a year, I'm able to give away larger chunks, and help so many more people than before.

We've contributed a lot of money to my alma mater, the University of Ottawa. They were creating an alumni building and they needed money to finish it. They asked if I would help; we did, and they wound up naming it after me. We've supported Fordham University, our son's alma mater, as well as the National Geographic Society. The Royal Canadian Geographical Society, whose geography bee I hosted for fifteen years, was on the verge of going belly up until we gave them some financial help. We also contribute here locally to a charity in the valley, Hope of the Valley Rescue Mission, for people who are homeless. They're building an eighty-bed facility in North Hollywood.

A cause that I have recently taken to heart through World Vision is helping Northern Kenya deal with the problem of female circumcision. A lot of the villages marry off their girls at a very young age, twelve and thirteen, and they circumcise them. We are trying to get them to change that, and we have constructed a boarding school for girls. The girls can leave home and live there, so they don't have to worry about being circumcised. They don't have to be married off. They are getting an education. And they are thriving.

We also adopted Kabeleka, a village in Zambia. It has about seventeen hundred residents. They used to get all their water from one well that animals drank from. Which meant that animals also defecated right there. It wasn't healthy for the people. And they had a two-room thatch hut as a school. So we adopted the village, and they built a new school made of blocks and mortar, with a big room for computers—even though they had no computers and they had no electricity. They built a medical facility, and they built three houses for teachers and medical personnel. And they drilled wells throughout the village.

It's always good
to receive a gift.

Collecting water
in Africa is the
responsibility of
women and girls.
Here, Emily takes
her turn drawing
water from the first
of eight wells we
drilled in Kabaleka.

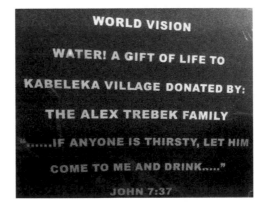

A few years ago, they asked us to come and see what had been accomplished. So Jeanie, the kids, and I went. We were greeted warmly, and they were singing. I couldn't understand a word they were saying, except "Trebek-ie! Trebek-ie!" They had a lovely banquet for us. They gave me a rooster. They gave me a goat. I realized I was going to have trouble getting them home, so I gave those away before we left.

Because it was such a success, the Zambian government was impressed and they brought in electricity from about a mile away. Since then, we have expanded the school and the medical facility, and they have built another home for the workers. Now pregnant women can go to the clinic and get a lot of prenatal childcare, ensuring they can give birth to healthier babies. Our names are tacked above some doorway. That's nice to know.

On the other side of the coin, once a charity gets hold of you, they don't let go. They keep coming back. What amazes me about charities these days is that I keep getting these requests in the mail: "It's time to renew your membership." Who made me a member? I sent you a donation. It was a donation. I did not join a club.

I got a mailer once saying, "Please help our friends, the draft horses." I thought, *Oh that's terrible. These horses are being maligned.* So I sent them a donation. Well, all of a sudden I'm on the list of animal lovers. Now I'm getting mailers from Save the Burros, Save the Mares, Save the Donkeys, Save the Tigers, Save the Lions, Dogs, and Cats. I mean, you name the animal with four legs and I'm on a list.

Another thing they do is send you an envelope with a dollar in it. So you feel bad. *Oh jeez, they sent me a dollar. I've gotta send*

In Mozambique with World Vision.

them something. Or they send an envelope with a stamp on it. So you say, "Well, I don't want them to waste their stamp." There are just so many ways in which they try to catch you. But it's always for good causes.

I have a joke about how many charities I contribute to. Most people contribute to charities because of personal involvement. Somebody has cancer in your family, so you're going to support a cancer organization. Or somebody died of a heart attack, so you'll support a heart association. I joke, because of my age, "I've recently been supporting the Alzheimer's Association. Well, I *think* I've been supporting the Alzheimer's Association. I'm not sure."

But, hey, there's a great need everywhere. And if you can afford it, go ahead and help them. You don't always have to spend a ton of money to make a difference in someone's life. I sponsor a child through World Vision—a young girl who has serious mental disabilities but is a sweet child. She's about thirteen now. For Christmas, World Vision said if we added a hundred dollars to our donation, they would buy a present for the girl and her family. I figured on clothes, but I got a notice the other day that they bought a mattress for the girl. She needed a mattress. They included a photo of her hugging her new mattress. We can make differences in simple ways and significant ways that don't cost much.

The Answer Is . . .

CAMARADERIE

I've also done a lot of work with the USO—the United Service Organizations. Just because I dropped out of military college after three days doesn't mean I don't appreciate the vital work of our service members. There are few things more admirable than a desire to help your country. Sure, there are some who join the military because they're hard-ass individuals and just like to lord it over other people. But, in my experience traveling the world with the USO, most military personnel are honorable people whose only motivation is to serve and protect. One of Matthew's schoolmates is a captain now. He's serving in Afghanistan. When I knew him in high school, he was just an ordinary kid who suddenly found his calling in the military and now serves our country and serves it well. And we're all very proud of him.

I've made about a dozen USO trips over the years. I show up to bases and give military personnel and their families a chance to participate in the *Jeopardy!* experience. They'll take the written test and I'll come out and chat with them. We did a testing once in Macedonia, about thirty miles from the Albanian border. There were only thirty people at the base there. No one had ever visited. Now, it's difficult for the USO to get a major rock star or a country

In Okinawa (*top*); kibitzing with the troops (*middle*);
shower time in Bosnia (*bottom left*); at sea (*bottom right*).

western star to go there because they often travel with a band and road crew. It's just not feasible. But for me and the *Jeopardy!* crew, it's only three or four people. We can do it.

I'm very appreciative of those sacrifices our men and women in uniform have made. And not only when we're involved in a conflict. That's one of the things that has always bothered me about the USO experience. You hear about all these celebrities who go entertain the troops when we're involved in a war. But where are they when we're at peace? There are certainly some committed stars who have gone on USO tours year after year, such as Toby Keith, Kellie Pickler, and Trace Adkins, to name a few. Our military members are still posted abroad. And some of them are hardship postings where they can't bring their family and they may be there for a couple of years. A lot of people don't understand how difficult it is for single men and women in the armed forces. Some of them stay on base all the time.

I recall visiting Bosnia and Herzegovina during the Bosnian War. I had to wear a flak vest and a helmet on my way to the shower, and I was told not to walk the streets of Sarajevo because there were snipers. Amid all this danger, I watched the American military erect temporary camps. I couldn't believe how fast they were able to build those camps.

That's one of the things that struck me most on my USO trips: the camaraderie aspect of it. When you are part of a group, then you have a common purpose. A common goal. Your resolve is increased and you can do marvelous, marvelous things together that would not be possible if you were left to your own devices. It's okay to think Rambo is great. But Rambo with a dozen other Rambos can accomplish tremendous things.

What Is . . .

AMERICA?

Last year, shortly after I announced my cancer diagnosis, I was notified that the Daughters of the American Revolution had chosen me for their Americanism Medal, which is presented to an American not born in this country. When I received the letter informing me of this honor, my initial reaction was *No way. It's not going to happen.* I'm not a big fan of sympathy votes, and I thought the DAR was being unusually generous and very sympathetic toward me because of my health condition. I felt very uncomfortable because of that. But then I reread the letter, and I noticed it was postmarked five days *before* I had made my announcement. Well, that changed everything, didn't it? Sympathy was no longer a factor. I said, "I will accept. Perhaps I even *deserve* this award." Not too sure about that. But I did accept it, and though I couldn't be at the ceremony in person, I recorded a taped speech that summarized my feelings about America. It went something like this:

"There are a lot of people in America who weren't born here, and some of them have major accomplishments. Think about it. Two former secretaries of state, Madeleine Albright and Henry Kissinger. A cofounder of one of the world's largest corporations,

Sergey Brin. Countless people in the show business and arts communities who have made major contributions to the culture in America. But we all have two things in common. First of all, most of us wanted to be here. We made a conscious decision to come to America because of the opportunities that were available here that were perhaps not available to us in our birth countries. And second, we have all come to deeply love this country.

"In my case, it happened quite naturally. My career prospered, I began experiencing the goodness of our society, then I met and fell in love with a beautiful young American girl from Long Island, New York. We got married in 1990, began raising two beautiful children, and I started to think about ways in which I could give back.

"Here's my idea of the true spirit of Americanism: it's an outstretched hand and a gentle voice that says, 'Through no fault of your own, you had a child who was born with serious birth defects. This is a major ordeal for you, one that can't be borne alone. Let us help you. Through no fault of your own, your job disappeared. It vanished. You can no longer support your family the way you did before. Oh, I know you got a replacement job, but it doesn't pay you anywhere near the salary you were earning prior to that event. You're in danger of losing your home. You can't afford health insurance. You certainly can't afford to send your kids to college. For that, they're going to have to take out big loans that they won't be able to repay for fifteen or twenty years after graduation. Let us help you.'

"It's that same hand reaching across two vast oceans, across international boundaries, and saying to foreign leaders, 'We understand that you govern your country very differently than we do here in the United States. You are not a democratic republic. Some of you repress your own citizens. Some of your people worship a superior being in ways that have become xenophobic and dangerous, but as long as you don't cross the line and threaten us, America will not raise a hand against you. In fact, we want to join hands with you to help solve some of the problems that are endangering people all around the planet.'

"Is the image of America that is projected abroad one that we feel comfortable with, or is there a way in which we can become better neighbors? I think all of us need to look at our country and figure out whether America lives up to the ideal America that we have in our minds and in our hearts. If it doesn't, if there's room for improvement—and there always is—let us act."

The Answer Is . . .

A CONSCIENCE

On *Jeopardy!*, we stay away from politics pretty well. We don't take overt positions with regard to liberalism or conservatism. We do this so well, in fact, that I'll get mail from Republicans thinking I'm a Republican, and I'll get mail from Democrats thinking I'm a Democrat. The truth is I'm an independent. I've voted for Republicans, and I've voted for Democrats. I vote for the person I feel is best suited to deal with the problems at that time.

What I look for in a politician is someone who cares about the people. *All* the people. Not just well-off people like me. If you're earning millions of dollars each year and have been doing so for the last ten years, you probably don't need any help financially. Earning an extra $200,000 because the federal government has reduced your taxes by 2.6 percent is not going to change your life. So why not pay that tax money and help the poor?

This seems like common sense to me. I don't see it as liberalism or conservatism. Unfortunately, in modern politics it has to be one or the other. Thanks in great part to twenty-four-hour cable news and social media, modern politics pits us against one another. It forces us to choose a side and has convinced us that our side is right and the other side is wrong. If you don't agree with me, you are my enemy. There is no room for compromise.

That's unfortunate. Because most of the great accomplishments of the world have not been made by people who were certain. The accomplishments have come about as a result of people who had doubts. "I don't know if this is going to work. I don't know how to solve this problem." And then they work on it. As opposed to, "Well, this is the way to solve the problem."

The comic Joey Bishop once told me, "Alex, as soon as somebody says to me they're absolutely sure of something, I immediately start doubting them." It's when you have doubt that people get together.

If you start off by saying, "Here's the way we're gonna solve it." And the other person says, "Maybe we could *try to* solve it this way." Well, which manner do you think is more likely to work? The one that allows for doubt or the one that begins with absolute certainty? And worse, if that certainty has no basis in fact and is being pushed by someone who doesn't have the mental capacity to adjust, then you're in deep trouble. And that's what we're seeing today.

We need a different approach. I often think of the lyrics from that old Burt Bacharach song sung by Jackie DeShannon: "What the world needs now is love, sweet love / It's the only thing that there's just too little of." As laudable as that is, love is not the be-all and end-all. We need more than that. What the world needs now is a *conscience*, in the business community and in politics.

Just look at how this is lacking in so many of our major businesses today. In the midst of a major pandemic, they are raising prices instead of making sacrifices for the common good. They are looking to protect their bottom line. I understand that, but I always thought we were the "United" States of America. That word seems to be getting short play these days. Aren't we supposed to rally together to help one another in times of disaster?

The politicians are no better. They fund aid for flood, tornado, and hurricane damage without denying those states the extra help we are providing at great cost. Yet some states are now suggesting we ignore the financial problems of New York and New Jersey and let them fend for themselves, even though they return more money to the federal coffers than they receive back in benefits. Is that really how we want to act? The politicians on both sides of the aisle pass regulations that they ignore themselves in order to cater to the public prior to the elections. They're *phumffing* around. They seem to be taking the short view rather than looking long term. I have one word of advice for both sides.

Enough!

The Answer Is . . .

A SINGLE STEP

When I came to America in 1973, the first thing that struck me, the first thing I noticed, is that it is one of the greatest therapeutic societies on the face of the earth. What I mean by *therapeutic* is this: a monster flood hits, a hurricane hits, a tornado hits, and we muster all of our services, all of our help, and we deal with that problem lickety-split. We're on it fast. But we're not a prophylactic society. We don't take steps beforehand to protect against problems that may come up. We wait for the shit to hit the fan, and then we act. We do not act beforehand. And that has always disappointed me about the United States. We have a perfect example of the consequences of this with the coronavirus.

We're seeing this also with global warming. Nineteen of the hottest years recorded on earth have occurred since 2001. These are facts, not fiction. For people to deny global warming is beyond me. The planet is in trouble. It didn't happen overnight. It's taken 150 years to get to where we are today. So, we're not going to remedy the problem in just a year or two. But we have to do something about it. Take coal: When you mine coal, you pollute the earth. When you burn coal, you pollute the earth. So you get a double dose of pollution from coal. I experienced this kind of pollution growing up in Sudbury. The fact that we're still doing it eighty years later is absolutely baffling to me.

There is a famous Chinese proverb: "A journey of a thousand miles begins with a single step." And that's what we need to do: take that single step so that future generations of Americans, our descendants, will be able to look back at us and say, "You know what? Our grandparents had some tough decisions to make. But because they made those decisions, the world is a better place in which to live and a safer one too."

What Is . . .

THE MUSK OX?

Another charitable cause I've been involved with is the protection of the musk ox. The musk ox has always been my favorite animal. That's because when they are threatened—and their main threat is from wolves up north—they form a circle with the calves and the cows in the middle and all the males facing outward, so their horns are projecting toward their enemy. That's how they protect the herd against attacks. No wolves can break that circle. Unless some poor musk ox in the circle decides he's going to start running. Once one ox starts to run, they all run. And when they're running, they are very vulnerable. Then the wolves can focus in on one and bring him down. But so long as they are committed to the circle, it is impenetrable. So long as they stand together, they are safe. There's a message there.

This has always touched me at a gut level. Sitting on a table here at home is a soapstone carving Jean gave me of a group of male musk oxen standing in a circle with their babies in the middle.

Years ago, a television producer discovered that the musk ox was my favorite animal. They were doing some reporting up in Alaska and they said, "You know what? There's a farm up there that raises musk oxen. Why don't you go up and do a report?" So

I did. I went up to Palmer, Alaska. While I was there, I offered to help them out. I gave them some money so they could put in new gates and fences. Now if you send in a donation to adopt a baby musk ox, you receive a certificate signed by the musk ox honorary parent, Alex Trebek.

Catching up with friends, my favorite animals.

The soapstone carving of musk oxen that Jean gave to me.

I know . . . that's a lot of denim. But wearing the
Canadian tuxedo is my birthright.

The Answer Is . . .

RIDING A HORSE

In addition to my passion for the musk ox, I also have a deep love for horses. I'm not sure where this interest comes from. If you walk around my house, I have tons of paintings and sculptures of horses. It wasn't done deliberately or consciously. When I was sitting on that sad-looking pony in Toronto as a child, I certainly wasn't thinking, *When I grow up, I want to own a seven-hundred-acre horse farm.* Though that's exactly what ended up happening.

In the mid-1980s, I'd loaned money to a friend who was setting up a winery.

When it came time to pay back the money, he said, "Instead, why don't you take an interest in the winery?"

"Good idea."

Ten years later, after losing two million dollars, I got out of the winery business. We were the only winery in California at the peak of wine growth in the state that lost money. I lost a lot of money and lost a friend. It's funny, money can change relationships so quickly. People will do things under financial pressure that destroy relationships.

The bank that was dealing with the winery had foreclosed on

this horse farm not far away. Seven hundred acres of prime land with a racetrack and barns and great pasture.

They came to me and said, "You know what you should do, Alex? You should buy this horse farm."

"I don't know anything about horses," I said.

"Not to worry," they replied, "there is a tenant who's leasing the horse farm now."

I went to look at it and fell in love with the place, and I bought it. Two months later, the guy who was leasing it said he wasn't going to renew. Now I had seven hundred acres of prime horse-training property that was going to be empty. So I got into the horse business. I started hiring advisers and breeders and a manager, and we began running the farm. We had some successes, but the business never did as well as it could've. So after about a decade, I sold the farm. I sold it just before the crash. I got lucky.

I didn't ride horses much myself. I did more riding at the winery than at the farm. We had horses for guests so they could take rides through the vineyards. One day, shortly after our wedding, Jeanie and I were out riding, and she went a little fast and fell off. She wasn't seriously hurt. But it was around that time that she got pregnant with Matthew. So we always joked that the reason Jeanie got pregnant was because she fell off the horse and that shook up her insides and that resulted in the pregnancy. That'll scare kids off from riding horses. They'll say, "Alex Trebek said I better not go horseback riding or I'll get pregnant."

What Is . . .

A SOUL MATE?

With Jean it just happened. Sometimes you know. Sometimes you look at something, you look at someone, and you know. I mean, you've heard stories of people who meet and decide within half an hour, "I knew this was going to be the person I'd end up with." And with Jeanie, that's how it was. I wasn't looking for love. But with Jean, I recognized at a gut level that here was someone who was going to complete me as a human being.

She was the bookkeeper for a friend—the same friend who chose not to date the lady with the grand piano. He was a business executive, and she was tending to his accounting. She was working on weekends because during the week she was studying at Pepperdine. I dropped in to visit my friend one Saturday, and he introduced me. She was the most charming person I had ever met; not only polite, but exuding a warmth that showed character and spirituality as well. And she was drop-dead gorgeous. I would see her at his place on other occasions too. One day, he invited me to a dinner party he was hosting, and I said, "I'll come if you ask Jean to come also." After that, we started dating. I don't know if Jeanie was as instantly certain about me as I was about her. I think at first she might've thought I was a bit of a jerk.

I do things on whims. That's how it was with our engagement. I had just come back from doing some World Vision work in Thailand. While I was there I found a sapphire-and-diamond ring. I had no purpose in mind in buying it. But then when I got back to LA, I decided that it would be an engagement ring.

I had also picked up a little toy truck on my trip—a little bamboo truck that was about the size of a Matchbox car. I told Jeanie, "I brought you a little dinky souvenir from Thailand." She opened the package, and there was this truck. Then she opened the back of the truck, and there was this sapphire-and-diamond ring. No note. Nothing. I asked her to marry me.

She ran crying from the room to go see my mom, who was living with me. Jean came back in the room a couple of minutes later and said yes. Interestingly enough, when Jeanie was growing up and had her little playhouse, her doll was always welcoming her husband home, and his name was Alex. How about that!

Then we had to tell her parents, Carol and Eric Currivan, who were my age. I hadn't met them yet. There is a twenty-four-year age difference between Jeanie and me. I was a bit concerned about it when we started dating, but those worries quickly disappeared. Still, I wondered how her dad would receive me. He was running a private investigation firm in New York, and he had arranged for a boat to host some family and friends for an engagement party. When Jeanie introduced me to him, he took one look at me and said, "I guess I won't be calling you 'son.'"

But we had a good relationship throughout his life. He would come and visit us here in Southern California. He liked nothing better than to rent a car and go driving. He loved to drive around

Jean and me at a charity event around the time we got married.

and sightsee. He died a few years ago. There were never any bad feelings or any animosity between us. Same with Jeanie's mom. She also visited us quite often and enjoyed a very special relationship with my mother. She's still alive, living in a senior-care facility in New York. So there were never any in-law problems. Once again, I've been very lucky.

Jeanie would not live with me before we got married. I found that interesting. There was a little bit of old-fashioned stuff going on. Her grandfather was a member of the Regency Club in Westwood. So we had the wedding there in April 1990. When the minister said, "Do you, Alex, take Jean to be your wife?" I said, "The answer is . . . 'Yes.'"

Leave it to me, always trying to go for a laugh. And I got one. Everybody cracked up.

As I write this, Jeanie and I have just celebrated our thirtieth anniversary. We had intended a romantic private getaway to celebrate—perhaps to our favorite place in England—but the coronavirus had other plans, so we simply stayed at home with Matthew and Emily. I ordered thirty bouquets of flowers that the kids spread throughout the house. A bottle of champagne and Emily's paella made for a perfect celebration. This might be one of the unintended positive consequences of COVID-19 . . . it has brought our family closer together.

In my office, near that framed check from the game show producer who stiffed me, I've got another framed image. Jeanie gave it to me. It's a line from our favorite movie, *Wuthering Heights*: "Whatever our souls are made of yours and mine are the same." That's the way I look at our relationship. We are one soul in two bodies.

The best day of my life.

Emily got it right.

My wife, the graffiti artist.

The Answer Is . . .

HAWORTH, ENGLAND

The first time I saw *Wuthering Heights*—the 1939 version starring Laurence Olivier and Merle Oberon—was probably in 1958 or 1959. It was at a drive-in theater in Sudbury. And it was raining—it started to rain during the film. I don't know why I remember that. I was alone. I'd borrowed my dad's car. It must've been a double feature or triple feature. I can't imagine that I would've gone by myself to see *Wuthering Heights*. But I just fell in love with the story. I tried to read the book but found the dialect very challenging. I never tired of watching the film, though.

I showed it to Jean when we were dating. She loved it too.

"Why don't we go there?" I said.

"Where?" she said.

"To England," I said. "To the Brontës' home."

It was located in the town of Haworth, in Yorkshire. It had been turned into a museum in the 1920s. So we went and had a wonderful time. We walked the moors in a pouring rainstorm and came across a beautiful abandoned sheep barn. Using a rock, we carved our names into one of the stone walls. Yes, I was responsible for graffiti in Yorkshire. It wouldn't be the last time.

After we got married, Jean and I went back to England. After we had Matthew, we returned, and we carved his name into the barn alongside ours. And after we had Emily, we made the trip yet again and carved her name into the barn.

In 2019, we went back once more, for Jean's birthday. We stayed in an enormous manor in Yorkshire set on twenty-four hundred acres. We visited the ruined Cistercian monasteries at Fountains Abbey and Rievaulx. I wasn't feeling well enough to walk the moors this time. However, the kids flew in and surprised Jeanie. Before we left, Emily said to her mom, "Let me see your phone to make sure you'll be able to make international calls when you're over there." But what she did was activate the tracking device on Jean's phone so that she would know exactly where we were at any time while we were over there. Emily flew from LA to New York to meet Matthew, and the two of them flew to Manchester, rented a car, and drove to Haworth. Jeanie and I were visiting the Brontë museum, and all of a sudden the kids came walking up the stairs and greeted us.

Perfect timing. Tears. It was wonderful.

The kids' surprise visit to Haworth and the Brontë Parsonage Museum.
(Rest assured, I'll get to my baldness later in the book.)

With Emily on set.

The Answer Is . . .

FATHERHOOD

Jean got pregnant with Matthew just three weeks after we were married. We wanted to have children, but we didn't think it would happen that quickly. If I remember correctly, Jean called to tell me she was pregnant just before I won my first Emmy. I was in New York. The ceremony was at Radio City Music Hall. In my acceptance I said something like, "I want to thank you for this. I just got a phone call from my wife telling me that she was expecting our first child. And I just heard the show has been picked up for next season. As soon as I leave this stage, I'm going to go outside and immediately buy a lottery ticket. Because today I'm *hot*."

When you get married and have sex, you're intelligent enough to realize one of the consequences is your wife could get pregnant. But it still doesn't prepare you for the incredible feeling of actually hearing the news.

Matthew's birth was hard for Jeanie. She probably should've stayed an extra day in the hospital. When we came home, it was Sunday. I carried the baby inside, and Jean went directly to bed to rest, and I took Matthew and put him on my chest and watched the Lakers game on television. We were all very happy and very satisfied with where we were on that day.

With Emily, I also found out right before I was about to do a show. It was the National Hockey League awards show in Toronto. And Jeanie called to let me know, "You're gonna get another one." Emily's birth was so much easier. With Emily, it was a piece of cake. I was taping a short-lived reboot of the game show *To Tell the Truth*, and word came down that Jeanie was going into labor. Mark Goodson was producing that show, and he said, "Go ahead. Just leave. Go." And he hosted the last two shows that were due to be taped. Yet he paid me for all five shows that week. He didn't deduct for the shows he hosted. Mark was a good guy in many ways.

The most challenging thing about fatherhood is that it introduced an element of fear into my life. When you're a bachelor, you do all kinds of dumb, daredevil things. You don't fear for your life too much. You don't worry about anything. But when you're married and have a family, you worry. If they go to school, you worry. If they're a little late to meet you, you worry. If they're not where they're supposed to be, you worry. And yet isn't it amazing how fathers—you never see mothers do this, only fathers—if they're out at a shopping mall with their kid, they will hide behind a post. Their child will start to cry, and then they'll pop out and say, "Oh, no, no, it's okay. Daddy's here." Guys are the only dorks who do that. Mothers don't do that because they realize it's traumatic. But guys—we're silly as all get-out.

It's not just the kids I worry about. It's Jeanie too. She goes on walks in the park near our house quite often. She'll go in the late afternoon. In the winter months, it gets dark early. I don't like her being up there when it's dark. It worries me.

So, yeah, having a wife and children introduces an element of fear into your life. And it changes your whole perspective on things that are important to you.

Celebrating Matthew's first communion.

The kids looking thrilled to be visiting Dad at work.

The Answer Is . . .

WORK-LIFE BALANCE

People often ask me how I juggle a career and family. It's not difficult because I only tape *Jeopardy!* two days a week. A total of forty-six days a year. Yeah, I know what you're thinking. I'm not exactly overworked. I have a lot of spare time. So I was able to go to all of Matthew's baseball games, for instance. I learned how to keep score, and I have all of those scoresheets saved. I have the baseball from his first over-the-wall home run as well as the ball that earned him his seventh RBI in the championship game. I'd go to all of Emily's basketball and volleyball games. Bryan Cranston and I helped out as assistant coaches. I'm lucky in that my work has not restricted the time I got to spend with my children. It has granted me more opportunities to be with them and, hopefully, to influence them.

We always had dinner together, which is very different from what I grew up with. I never had dinner with my dad. Just my mom. With Matthew and Emily, it was always dinner at the same time every night. I don't think that was an intentional choice. I don't think I was reacting to the way I was raised and consciously trying to do things differently. To be honest, I followed Jean's lead on parenting. She is the calming influence. She has a more understanding personality. She's not as rigid. And when you have one half of the relationship that's a softening agent, if you will, that takes the sting out of discipline and it helps tremendously. It keeps the other partner from going wacko and overdoing punishment or whatever.

After dinner the kids would go do their homework or play games in what we call the "Play-Doh Room," right next to the kitchen. They didn't watch *Jeopardy!* very often. It was not must-see television for them. They knew their father was the host of a television quiz show. But they'd say, "I'm doing my homework now, so I'm not gonna watch."

What Is . . .

LOSS?

Dad died soon after Elaine and I got divorced. Sometimes, when one's parent dies, suddenly there are unresolved issues that prey on the child for years afterward. There was none of that with my dad. We were at peace with each other and had a great relationship and even though Mom and Dad had been apart for decades, they remained close. Mom flew to Sudbury to be with him shortly before he passed away.

My sister, Barbara, died in 2007 of breast cancer. She married the boyfriend she'd moved to Los Angeles for. Then they got divorced and she married the man next door. Yet she stayed friendly with her ex-husband. So there's consistency in the Trebek households.

I was at her bedside when she passed. My mother was there, and so was Barbara's husband. I turned to my mom and said, "Barbara's gone."

"What?" she said.

"Yeah," I said. "She just went."

I was also with my mom when she died a few years later. Jeanie was in New York visiting her dad, who was not well. I was sleeping in the guesthouse, which we had set up as a hospice for Mom. She was downstairs in a hospital bed in what used to be the dining area. I was upstairs in her bedroom. I woke up during the night, looked down over the railing into the dining area, and realized she was gone. She must have passed a few minutes before I awoke, because something had roused me. Then I went down, and I called the number for the hospice people, and they had a nurse come over and deal with all of the paraphernalia. With morphine, you have to smash the vials—all that stuff. I called Jeanie and my son in New York, and I called Emily. Then I called the crematorium. I had already made the arrangements, just as I had done for my dad years earlier.

As I said before, Mom and I had resolved everything and were comfortable in our relationship and the love we had for each other. She would walk the property with our dog, Wilbur, and we would sit together on the outside swing and just chat. Losing her didn't devastate me. I had come to terms with it pretty well. And so had Mom. She was ninety-five.

She had even given away her beloved cat. She had this big Maine coon cat named Happy. It was so loving and always rubbing up against her legs when she walked around. She started to get nervous that she would trip and fall and break a hip or a leg. So, shortly before she died, she gave it to one of *Jeopardy!*'s supervising producers, Rocky Schmidt.

So I don't have a lot of ghosts. I don't have any bad memories that affect my life. It's all good. Sure, I think of Mom and Dad and Barbara often. Sure, there are sad moments. But I never think of them and say, "I wish we had resolved this or resolved that." There was nothing to resolve. There was no unfinished business. It's all good stuff.

A nice visit
with Dad.

Mom visiting Dad
in the hospital.

With my mom
and sister.

The Answer Is . . .

GREAT COLLEAGUES

Our writers and researchers have been with *Jeopardy!* for so long, I'll often joke that working for the show is an annuity. They are constantly working on questions. We've developed a large backlog over the years. In fact, one of our original writers, a guy named Steven Dorfman, died in 2004 after working on the show for nearly twenty years. He wrote something like fifty thousand clues during that time. We're probably still using some of them.

The writers, God bless them, are really sharp. They've won a lot of Emmys, and they deserve them. They can take a mundane fact and make it very entertaining. They once came up with the category "When the Aztecs Spoke Welsh." The category's clues were made up of Aztec words and Welsh words. It scared the daylights out of me. It was a tongue twister's delight. I spent a great deal of time preparing to pronounce all the words. In the production meeting, I said, "Damn, you guys gave me some tough stuff in this category."

After a brief pause, they said, "Did you look at the date?"

At the top of each game sheet is the date when that game will air. The airdate of that game was April 1. So it was an April Fools' joke on me. I was really ticked at them because I'd put in a lot of time working on all those words and getting the right diacritical marks so that I'd give them the correct pronunciation. I've always thought we should have done it as a real category. Because the clues were valid. Of course, if I screwed it up, I'd have to come after them with a baseball bat.

You could replace me as the host of the show with anybody and it would likely be just as popular. Hell, after thirty-six years with me, it might even be more popular. The show might be even more appreciated than it is with me as host. This goes back to what I said earlier about always insisting I be introduced as the host rather than the star. I try to be intelligent enough with regard to my profession to know what the most important elements of the show are. Right at the top are the writing and the clues.

With Jean in Whitby, England. Whenever
we travel, I'm always looking out for interesting
facts that might be turned into clues.

Who Is . . .

DRACULA?

During our last trip to Haworth, when the kids surprised Jeanie for her birthday, we took a day trip to a little fishing village on the northeast coast of England called Whitby. Whenever I'm traveling—whether for vacation or for World Vision—there's always some bit of information that I pick up and make a mental note of and later transmit to the writing staff. This was one of those occasions.

When I got home, I asked the writers: "What do you guys know about Whitby?"

They said nothing. They were stumped.

"Well," I said, "that's where Dracula first lands in England in Bram Stoker's novel."

When we were sightseeing, we came across a plaque that commemorated this.

"Great," the writers said. "That's a clue. We'll work that into the show."

We use so much material on our show. It pleases me if I can come up with something original to pass on to the writers. I don't have such a big ego that I'm going to get my nose out of joint if they don't accept my suggestions, but it always makes me happy when they do. It's the same with regard to rulings from the judges. I'll express my opinion, sometimes forcefully, about whether a ruling was correct. But if they don't accept my opinion, I'm not going to go in the corner and sulk. I get past it immediately. We've got a show to do. I've always believed what Mark Goodson instilled in me: if it is a good idea, it doesn't matter where it's coming from. My prime allegiance is always trying to improve the program. If you've got a better idea than mine, I'm not going to let my ego get in the way and prevent the powers that be from accepting an idea because it didn't come from a higher-level employee. In our business, you have to get your priorities right.

Once, it occurred to me that there had been a lot of different actors who portrayed Wyatt Earp. Will Geer played Wyatt Earp in *Winchester '73*. James Garner. Kevin Costner. Kurt Russell. I said, "What if that was a category?" So they wrote it, and it played well.

There are some categories that have failed, sure. And some that have succeeded marvelously well. And there's no way of knowing. It all depends on the three contestants who are on the show that particular day. You have a category that is dynamite. *Dy-no*-mite, as Jimmie Walker used to say. And it dies. No one comes up with the correct response. Played well in our production meeting but not in the taping. Those three players didn't get it. Three other players might've mopped the floor with it. You never know.

A recent example of this, which ended up going viral, was a category we did all about football. Not all the clues were that difficult, but the three players who happened to be in that game clearly knew nothing about football. This was perhaps obvious given it was the last category left on the board that round. The contestants had been avoiding it all game, but now they had no choice. Here were the answers*:

$200: YOUR CHOICE: DO OR DON'T NAME THIS PLAY IN WHICH THE QB RUNS THE BALL & CAN CHOOSE TO PITCH IT TO ANOTHER BACK

$400: TOM LANDRY PERFECTED THE SHOTGUN FORMATION WITH THIS TEAM

$600: BY SIGNALING FOR ONE OF THESE, A RETURNER CAN REEL IN A KICK WITHOUT FEAR OF GETTING TACKLED

$800: THESE "PENALTIES" ARE SIMULTANEOUS VIOLATIONS BY THE OFFENSE & DEFENSE THAT CANCEL EACH OTHER OUT

$1000: THIS DEFENSIVE LINE TOOK THE MINNESOTA VIKINGS TO FOUR SUPER BOWLS

The contestants didn't get a single clue right. They didn't even ring in. Not once. Nonetheless, we all had a good time with it, and it ended up being one of the funniest moments on our show. To follow that up, this season I suggested we do a category about the signals the referees use to indicate penalties. My idea was that I would perform the signals as part of the clues. I suggested clues and even sketched them out on paper, exhibiting each hand or arm movement. Thankfully, the contestants had better luck with this football category. But again, it all comes down to what you know, even the things that might seem out of left field. Yes, I know I'm mixing a baseball reference with football.

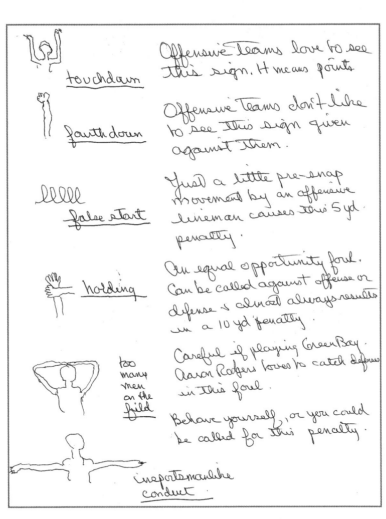

touchdown — Offensive Teams love to see this sign. It means points

fourth down — Offensive Teams don't like to see this sign given against them.

false start — Just a little pre-snap movement by an offensive lineman causes this 5 yd penalty.

holding — An equal opportunity foul. Can be called against offense or defense & almost always results in a 10 yd penalty.

too many men on the field — Careful if playing Green Bay. Aaron Rodgers loves to catch defenses in this foul.

unsportsmanlike conduct — Behave yourself, or you could be called for this penalty.

My sketch for the hand-signal football clues.

What is a touchdown?

What is fourth down?

What is a false start?

What is holding?

What is too many men on the field?

One of the little joys I have with some *Jeopardy!* contestants is challenging them with relatively obscure bits of information. For example, "These are the four defendants in the film *Judgment at Nuremberg.*" Now, I happen to know that. And I've known that for a long time. I don't know why those names have stuck with me, but I happen to know them. Nobody else does. Nobody else cares. But if that came up on a show and you didn't know, so what. Don't feel bad about it.

Emil Hahn, Ernst Janning, Friedrich Hofstetter, and Werner Lampe. Just in case you were wondering.

---

* And here are the correct responses to those football clues. How many did you get right?

$200: WHAT IS AN OPTION PLAY?
$400: WHO ARE THE DALLAS COWBOYS?
$600: WHAT IS A FAIR CATCH?
$800: WHAT ARE OFFSETTING PENALTIES?
$1000: WHO ARE THE PURPLE PEOPLE EATERS?

The Answer Is . . .

IMPROVISATION
AND PREPARATION

The successful game show hosts are all very good at ad-libbing. They don't need a script. They may need cue cards to help them with the next element of the show itself, but they're able to converse with the contestants and draw the contestants out and get funny responses or create something funny out of an off-the-wall comment made by a contestant.

Bob Eubanks, for instance—he called the other day, wishing me well. He hasn't been on the air hosting a game show in years, but he's still well-remembered. He used to get a lot of mileage just out of a look. As a host, you learn how to do that. You learn that a pause, just a pause, can be worth its weight in gold. Because a contestant will say something, and you pause, you look at the camera, and sometimes you don't even have to say anything. You don't have to make the comment. The viewers at home or the studio audience, they make the transition for you. They get the joke. They laugh. And you just continue. That's part of being a good host. And there are some guys who do it better than others. Peter Marshall was a master on *The Hollywood Squares*. You have to be aware of stuff like that.

Before the show starts, I'll stand backstage and try to think of what I'm going to say when I walk out. Because I don't want to be repetitious with regard to the opening of the show, I try to come up with different ways of welcoming the audience. If it's Valentine's Day, I'll open with "Happy Valentine's Day, everyone." Or if the contestants are all from the East Coast, I'll open with "Today, we've got three contestants all from the Eastern Seaboard." Yet because of our taping schedule, there's usually a couple of months between when we tape the shows and when they air. So my banter can't be too topical. If a contestant is a fan of a particular football team, for instance, I can't say, "They're looking good this year." Because by the time the show runs they might be in last place in the standings. So I have to be a little more broad.

Still, you try to find something, some element that might be of interest to your viewers. Your job is to keep it fresh, keep it alive, keep your viewers interested in what's going on. I don't plan what I'm going to say fifteen or twenty minutes in advance. Because twenty minutes earlier I'm wrapping up the previous show. So I try to be creative there. And that puts a little pressure on me and fires up the adrenaline. The same is true when acknowledging contestants' responses. There are only so many ways of saying "Correct" or "That's right," so it's easy to get into a rut and keep repeating the same thing.

What I do has a lot in common with being an actor on Broadway. We both do the same show night after night, and we have to find new ways to make it unique and interesting to ourselves. I'm sure if you were to ask some of our successful Broadway actors, "Has there ever been a night where you just, out of wanting to have fun and maybe being the only one who was aware of it, just started doing things a tad off, a tad differently? In the way you were saying

(Clockwise from top left): The game-show-host gang:
Peter Marshall, Tom Kennedy, Ralph Edwards, me, Jack
Narz, Charles Nelson Reilly, and Betty White.

the lines or in the movements?" Some actors might say, "No, every night is different because there's a different audience." Wrong! It's the same audience. They just happen to have different faces, that's all. We have a different audience every time we tape the show, and the people ask the same questions—*the same questions*—in the commercial breaks. So it's the same audience. How, then, do you keep it fresh for yourself as a host? And if you can do that, hopefully you're keeping it fresh for the audience too. Though you never want to inject too much of yourself into the show. You never want to become a stand-up comic trying to take over. But I do have fun in those commercial breaks.

Here are some of the questions that I hear from the audience for the "first time" hundreds of times a year:

What's your favorite color?
Gray, it matches my personality.

How would you do as a contestant?
Against my peers (people in a coma), I'd do fine. But a good thirty-year-old would clean my clock.

If you weren't hosting *Jeopardy!*, what would you be doing?
I think I'd be a good pope. I look good in white.

Which three famous people would you have liked to see on the show?
Ava Gardner, because she was so beautiful. Mark Twain, because he was so bright. And Ava Gardner again, just because she's Ava Gardner.

What's your favorite book?

Growing up, it was *The Moonstone* by Wilkie Collins. Now, it's *The Razor's Edge* by W. Somerset Maugham.

What are your favorite *Jeopardy!* categories?

Geography . . . Movies . . . Movies about Geography.

What's the favorite place you traveled to with the show?

There's so many: Machu Picchu, the Galápagos, Israel, Petra . . .

Is there any place still on your bucket list?

The Potala Palace in Tibet. We were supposed to go there a few years ago, but the Chinese government was worried about unrest, so the trip was canceled. I'd still like to get there.

Who do you think should replace you?

Someone younger. Someone brighter. Someone funnier. Betty White.

When we wrap each taping, I tell audiences my hope is that having been there to see how we do it, to see what we go through, to see me screw up and redo a clue because I've misread it, will add to their enjoyment from now on when they watch the show at home. Because you're used to seeing it a certain way at home, without knowing the nuts and bolts. You just see the car in the showroom. And now all of a sudden you're on the road. It's Ford versus Ferrari. You're going 160 miles per hour. The game moves incredibly fast. I often won't know who's in the lead until I look up and see their

Fielding questions from the audience.

scores. Sometimes our stage manager will come up after the first commercial and say, "We're forty-five seconds long." And so in the next segment I'll try to move things along more swiftly. Or he'll say we're running ahead of schedule and I'll have to stretch. I'm driving the show. It's my job to give it more gas or put my foot on the brake. I have to keep the show moving, guide it, present an environment in which the contestants are going to be performing at their very best. Because that's how the show succeeds.

It's not quite the same as just looking at it and saying, "What a lovely car." When you watch at home, you think, "What a lovely show." But when you watch it live in the studio, you see how intricate and impromptu so much of it is.

While improvisation is important to the show, so is preparation. You can only improvise if you are well prepared.

We tape two days a week, five shows each day. On tape days I come into the office at 6:00 a.m. First, I'll grab breakfast. For years, my breakfast of choice was a Snickers and a Diet Coke. Then my doctor lectured me about changing that. So now it's a Kit Kat and a Diet Pepsi. Then I'll go over all the games that we'll be taping that day. I have newspaper-size broadsheets of all the answers and questions printed out, and I read through each clue and response to familiarize myself with the words so that I don't make too many mistakes in pronun . . . pronunci . . . pronucia . . . in saying words properly. Five games. Sixty-one clues a game. That's 305 clues. It takes about an hour and a half to go through them all. Then I go review the day's *Los Angeles Times* to make sure I am up on all the current news. Not good for a host to state incorrect facts on a show like ours. Then, if I have time, I do their crossword puzzle.

At 9:00 a.m. I go into a production meeting with our writers and producers, and together we review all the games to make sure that a subject or clue in one game isn't too similar to a subject or clue in another game. The games are selected randomly, as are the contestants who play in any given game, which protects us from any concern that it might appear we're favoring one contestant over another. When I'm first reviewing the clues I'll circle any that I think need to be discussed with the group. Sometimes I'll also suggest changing the wording of a clue if I feel like it can be improved. We may make a last-minute change based on something that's just happened in current events, which might make a clue out-of-date, or inappropriate. I always keep a dictionary handy, and if I can't find what I'm looking for in the dictionary I'll turn to our crack team of researchers. I've often said that even if I retire from hosting the show, I would love to keep coming in on tape days just to participate in these morning meetings. Lots of talk. Lots of jokes.

After the production meeting, I go to makeup and put on my suit. We do three shows with one audience, then we take a lunch break and tape the last two shows with a different audience. Even during shows I'm continuing to make notes on the clue sheets, crossing off clues as I read them to ensure I don't read any clues that have already been played. For this I use a Crayola crayon—because it's the writing implement that makes the least amount of noise and won't be picked up by my microphone.

We finish taping around five in the evening. It's basically an eleven-hour day. Yes, *Jeopardy!* is a game. But to all of us who work on the show, it's a job—one we take seriously.

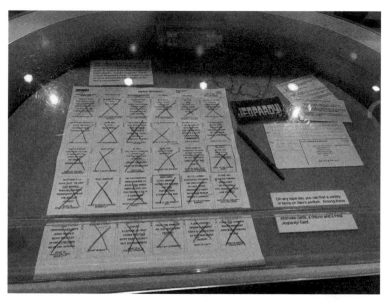

What my finished "script sheet" looks like after a completed game. This one happens to be from the last game of Ken Jennings' historic run.

7:30 a.m. to 8:45 a.m.: Receiving
the five "show scripts" for the day
from head writer Billy Wisse.

9:00 a.m. to 10:00 a.m.:
Production meeting.

10:30 a.m. to 11:15 a.m.:
Hair and makeup.

11:15 a.m. to 12:00 p.m.: Ready
for the first show of the day.

12:00 p.m. to 12:15 p.m.: Off to
change into a new suit. (The returning
champion also changes clothes so that
people at home don't wonder why they
only have one outfit for the week.)

12:15 p.m. to 1:00 p.m.: Announcer
Johnny Gilbert kicks off the second show.

1:00 p.m. to 1:15 p.m.: Another suit change before the third show.

1:15 p.m. to 2:00 p.m.: Taking a moment to gather myself before show number three—as I do before every show.

2:00 p.m.: Lunch break. I usually get the soup of the day or sushi.

3:45 p.m.: Last suit of the day before the fifth and final show.

3:45 p.m. to 4:15 p.m.: Consulting with the judges.

5:00 p.m.: Happy to be heading home.

Frank Spangenberg heading into his fifth game, during which he'd win a then-record-setting $30,600. (The current single-day winnings record was notched in 2019 by James Holzhauer: $131,127.)

What Is . . .

THE FIVE-GAME RULE?

From the beginning of *Jeopardy!*, there was a rule that after a contestant won five games in a row, they retired as an "undefeated champion." This was in part a response to the quiz show scandals of the 1950s. *Jeopardy!* didn't want it to seem as if any one player had a suspicious advantage or that the producers had a vested interest in a particular contestant continuing to win. Of course, as I mentioned earlier, the show itself came about in response to those scandals, with Julann Griffin's suggestion that one way to win back the public's trust in quiz shows was to provide contestants with the answers and ask them to provide the questions. Thus *Jeopardy!* was born.

The drawback of the five-game rule was that it didn't always allow the audience to emotionally invest in the contestants. Just as you got to know a contestant and really started rooting for them, they were forced to stop playing. For instance, Frank Spangenberg was a New York City police officer who attracted a lot of attention in 1990. He was from Flushing, Queens, and had this great handle-bar mustache. He set a one-game record of $30,600 and a five-game record of $102,597. But then he was done.

Granted, even after just those five shows Frank became

somewhat of a celebrity. When he returned to the show some years later for a champions tournament, he told the story of taking a trip to the Grand Canyon. He was standing by himself on the south rim admiring the view. A woman came out of the woods behind him.

"Oh my God," she said.

"Yeah," Frank said, assuming she was referring to the view. "I feel the same way."

"Oh my God, you're Frank Spangenberg," she said. "I know you from *Jeopardy!*"

Frank joked that his notoriety made doing undercover police work impossible.

In 2003, as we readied to begin taping our twentieth season, our executive producer, Harry Friedman, suggested doing away with the five-game rule. Our two supervising producers, Rocky Schmidt and Lisa Broffman, were initially concerned. What if you got a contestant on a hot streak who was unlikable, who the audience couldn't stand to watch? But we decided to take a chance, and it was probably the best thing that happened to the show.

Who Is . . .

KEN JENNINGS?

Shortly after we got rid of the five-show rule, the records for con-secutive wins quickly started to fall. First, a taxi driver, bartender, and student from State College, Pennsylvania, named Sean Ryan won six games. Then a writer from Washington, D.C., named Tom Walsh won seven games. All of us who worked on the show thought, *Wow! Seven games straight!* We were so impressed. And then toward the very end of that season, a thirty-year-old software engineer from Salt Lake City, Utah, arrived. His name was Ken Jennings.

When I think of Ken, I think of a quality human being. Ex-tremely bright—that goes without saying. Someone who's not out to impress you. Somebody I can be very simpatico with because I think we're the same type of person. We're comfortable in our own skin and comfortable in dealing with other people and don't feel we have to go out and impress or make a mark. He's somebody I genuinely liked as a contestant on the program.

About the time he won his fifth game in a row, I knew he was something special. I knew the guy was going to be a force to reckon with. It turned out that Ken was on the show for sixteen weeks, winning seventy-four straight games and more than $2.52 mil-lion. Soon I started running out of questions to ask him during the interview segment of each show. So he would suggest things. I think he even made up some stories, such as how he likes airline food. He's got a great sense of humor, but it's not an out-there kind of humor. Reactionary humor. Not I'm-going-to-tell-you-a-joke humor. Maybe we had that in common from the get-go, or maybe we just developed this camaraderie because of the length of time he spent with me on the program.

One common misconception about *Jeopardy!* is that I become friendly with the contestants and have a great deal of interaction with them. That's not the case. There's no time. Because we are taping five shows a day, we only have fifteen minutes between each game. I go back to my dressing room, change my suit, get my makeup touched up, then come back out for the next game. The only opportunity I have to interact with contestants is during the actual game.

Even if I did have more time to spend with them, I wouldn't. I wouldn't want anyone to think I was favoring one contestant over another or that there was some hanky-panky going on. I've heard plenty of stories like that about other hosts over the years. On one game show that will remain nameless, there was a very attractive female contestant. A few weeks after she appeared on the show, one of the staff members called her home to verify that she received her winnings. They were surprised to hear the host of the show answer the phone. That never happened on *Jeopardy!*

But if you've got somebody with you on the show for sixteen weeks and you are interacting during the conversation segments, that all mounts up. That's thirty-seven hours Ken and I spent together. We got to know each other and feel comfortable with each other. Letterman joked about us taking out a license and moving to Massachusetts and getting married.

Ken had taped around forty shows before any of them aired. We weren't 100 percent sure people were going to like watching a player be so dominant. "Good God, why are we watching this guy?" So that was sort of an unknown quantity. But then obviously the fans got invested and continued to tune in. Over the course of Ken's run, the show's ratings increased 22 percent compared to the same period the year before. And for several weeks during that time we were the highest-rated syndicated program on television.

Obviously I knew that Ken's reign would come to an end eventually. Though I must admit I never expected it to happen the way it did. Going into Final Jeopardy!, he was in the lead with $14,400. The second-place contestant, a real estate agent from Ventura, California, named Nancy Zerg, had $10,000. The other contestant was in the red and didn't make it to Final Jeopardy! The Final Jeopardy! category was "Business and Industry"; the clue was:

MOST OF THIS FIRM'S 70,000 SEASONAL WHITE-
COLLAR EMPLOYEES WORK ONLY 4 MONTHS A YEAR

Since Nancy was in second place, we revealed her response first:

WHAT IS H&R BLOCK?

She was correct. She wagered $4,401, which put her ahead of Ken by a single dollar. Then I went to Ken for his response:

WHAT IS FEDEX?

Oh my God, I thought. *He's done.*

Before I even had a chance to read it out loud, the audience gasped in shock. The camera then cut to Nancy, who put her hands over her mouth in utter disbelief. Later, when I thought about that moment, what amazed me was that before we revealed Ken's answer on his monitor, I didn't notice anything different about him. There wasn't the slightest change in his face or body language that indicated what happened. I always thought that was a sign of what a class act he was. He was a true professional and great sportsman until the very end. He turned to Nancy and not only shook her hand but gave her a hug. I got the sense that he was genuinely happy for her.

"Congratulations," I said to Nancy, "you are indeed a giant-killer!"

The studio audience rose to their feet and clapped—a standing ovation for both players.

There was definitely a sadness. I had tears in my eyes. It just all happened so quickly. Ken lost. I said something like, "Ken, you're going away with a lot of money" and, to the viewers at home, "We'll see you tomorrow." The show ended. I remember thinking, "Ken's gone. My buddy. My pal. This was getting to be *The Ken and Alex Show*." To give viewers more closure, we brought Ken back before the next game so we could say a proper goodbye.

It was a great reminder about the importance of the categories on *Jeopardy!* There's always the possibility that somebody will get lucky when their categories happen to come up and they're able to take advantage. It doesn't matter who you are. The categories are the great equalizer. Nancy Zerg experienced this herself. After beating Ken, she lost in her very next game.

A software engineer from Salt Lake City, Utah . . .

A professional sports gambler from Las Vegas, Nevada . . .

Who Is . . .

JAMES HOLZHAUER?

As with Ken Jennings, I knew very early that James Holzhauer was something special. On his fourth show, he set a new one-day winnings record. He'd come up with a correct response and I'd think, *How the hell did he know that?* I found his thirty-two game winning streak so compelling that, like the rest of America, I would tune in every night at home to watch.

Of course, you can't discuss James without first mentioning Chuck Forrest. Chuck appeared on *Jeopardy!* in 1985, during my second season hosting the show. In some ways, he invented the strategy of jumping around on the gameboard rather than working through each category from top to bottom. In fact, it became known as the "Forrest Bounce." Chuck set what was, at the time, a total earnings record of $72,800. Chuck was incredibly likable, and held several *Jeopardy!* records for many years. But because of the five-game rule, he never became a household name the way James and Ken did.

James used the "Forrest Bounce" a bit differently than Chuck. For Chuck, it was more of a defensive tactic. He used it primarily to keep his opponents off-balance so that they could never settle into a rhythm and get comfortable. Chuck has said that he felt that bouncing from category to category allowed him to know a split second before his opponents what the next subject matter was going to be. James used it more as an offensive tactic. He went for the highest-value clues and amassed as much money as possible, not only to put the game more quickly out of reach for his opponents but also to win. Which is why he almost always went all-in on Daily Doubles and never shied away from betting the farm. James also just wanted to take home as much money as he could. That might seem obvious. "Doesn't every contestant?" you might say. What I've found is that the majority of contestants care more about winning the game. The money is wonderful, but what they *really* want is to be able to call themselves a *Jeopardy!* champion. Eventually the money runs out, but the bragging rights of saying "I won on *Jeopardy!*" last forever. James has the utmost respect for the game and is a terrific champion, but his aim was to amass as much money as possible. Remember, he was introduced on the show as a professional gambler.

Now, I have often said that I'm not a fan of the strategy of starting at the bottom of the gameboard. It has always bothered me when contestants adopt the tactic of going to higher-priced clues before they know what the category is about. The gameboard is arranged the way it is to help the player. Some categories are too hard to decipher until you've seen the first couple of clues in order. By jumping deep into a category, it may be that no one will be able to respond to the clue and that money will go unclaimed. However, James had the knowledge to back up that strategy—the knowledge and the guts.

Ken has said James changed the way the game is played. That's

With Chuck Forrest in 1985.

why Ken and Brad Rutter—*Jeopardy!*'s highest-earning contestant ever—had to change their strategy in the recent "Greatest of All Time" games. The strategy of slow and steady and betting $5,000 on a Daily Double wasn't going to work. They had to adopt James's strategy and use it against him. That was the only way they were going to beat him. And Ken did.

James Holzhauer, Ken Jennings, and Brad Rutter during 2020's "Greatest of All Time" competition.

What Is . . .

STRATEGY?

My motto has been, in terms of dangerous situations, until you know what the hell's going on, don't do anything. Bend your toes into the ground like talons and don't move until you figure out what's happening here. Is there a danger? Where is there safety? What should I be afraid of? And as soon as you figure it out, then, feet, do your stuff. To me, there's no plus to running around just for the sake of running around, until you figure out what's going on. And the same thing is true as a contestant on *Jeopardy!*

You came up with a couple of incorrect responses. Okay, take it easy. Settle down. Take a deep breath. Don't try to make up for it on the next clue if you're not 100 percent sure. A lot of contestants try a little too hard and guess at clues they shouldn't. There are going to be thirty more clues coming up. Then another thirty clues. You'll get a chance. Wait for your chance. If it's a category you don't feel confident in, lay back for a while. Maybe the first person to ring in gets it wrong, and maybe the second person to ring in gets it wrong. Even if you don't know that much about that subject, two possible responses that might have occurred to you have now been eliminated. So now maybe you can take a chance. "Oh, hello, I just made $1,600. Thank you very much."

And don't immediately jump down to the $2,000 clue—unless you're James Holzhauer and you're so bright you can get almost all of those correctly. Why place extra pressure on yourself? The game contains enough pressure to satisfy any player. Don't make it more challenging than it is. I always recommend starting at the top of a category, because sometimes the category titles don't even tell you what it is.

On the other hand, when it comes to Final Jeopardy!, it never ceases to amaze me how conservative contestants will be with their bids. When there is no other alternative but to bet everything they've got, when that's the only way they will win, many still won't do it. The difference between second place and third place is a thousand dollars. If you finish in second place you get $2,000. If you finish in third you get $1,000. (Fans of the show's early days will remember the runners-up prizes included Lee Nails, "delicious low-calorie meat" from Mr. Turkey, and Tinactin Antifungal Cream—use only as directed!) Bet as much as you can or need to in order to win the game. There have been books written about *Jeopardy!* strategy, and several theories out there about wagering in Final Jeopardy! But, for me, it always comes back to the Kaiser Wilhelm line, which was one of General Patton's favorite quotes: *"L'audace, l'audace, toujours l'audace."* Audacity, audacity, always audacity.

MERCURY

QUEEN

WE WILL ROCK YOU

Here are three 2019 categories that could take you down many different paths.

EDDIE

A sportswriter from Reston, Virginia . . .

Who Is . . .

EDDIE TIMANUS?

We've had a number of physically-challenged individuals as contestants on *Jeopardy!* If you can pass the test, you can be a player on our show—that's always been our criteria. One of those contestants who made a big impression on me was Eddie Timanus back in 1999. Eddie was a sportswriter from Reston, Virginia. He was the first blind contestant to compete on the show. The only accommodations we made: we provided him with a braille readout of the categories, and we also gave him a keyboard that he used to type his responses for Final Jeopardy! Eddie became a five-game winner and an inspiration to all. As a bonus at the time for becoming a five-time champion, Eddie also received two new Chevrolet Camaros. When asked about the cars, he remarked what was so odd about that was that he could only drive one of them at a time. Nice sense of humor Eddie has.

A few years later, he came back to compete in the Battle of the Decades tournament. In an interview that aired during that program, Eddie said something that really moved me:

"People ask me, 'How did you do it? Wasn't it a disadvantage for you?' And I say, 'Well, maybe, but this is just my life. This is who I am.'" We also found out that in the intervening years, Eddie had been contacted by a teacher who wanted to ask him about using *Jeopardy!* in her classroom. Eddie consulted with her, and she is now his wife and they have a wonderful son.

Who Is . . .

CINDY STOWELL?

In 2016, a contestant named Cindy Stowell made her *Jeopardy!* debut. Cindy was a forty-one-year-old science content developer from Austin, Texas. She won six games, over the course of which she shared with viewers personal details such as how she loved to crochet but was still getting the hang of it; she'd recently knitted a baby blanket for a friend that turned out to be more of a queen-size comforter. However, what was not discussed on the show was that Cindy had stage IV colon cancer. After Cindy passed the online test, she was invited to attend one of our regional in-person auditions. She responded and asked the contestant coordinators if we could speed up the audition process and that if she were picked to be on the show, it might have to happen soon because she didn't have long to live.

As the *New York Times* reported in her obituary, she taped four games on August 31 in intense discomfort and pain. She was nauseated, had a fever, and experienced so much abdominal pain that she required painkillers. Only myself, the producers, and the contestant staff knew about her illness. The other contestants did not. They just thought Cindy was under the weather or nervous. The

A science content developer from Austin, Texas . . .

medicine she took delayed Cindy's reaction time. And yet despite all this, she kept winning.

After that first day, the show took a scheduled break in taping. Cindy was hospitalized for a week with a blood infection. But when we resumed taping in mid-September, she was back to defend her title. She won two more games. In one of her wins, she was in the red in Double Jeopardy! and trailed her two opponents by $6,000 yet managed to come back.

Cindy died on December 5, just a week before her games aired. Prior to that, we sent her a DVD of her games so she at least got to see herself on the show.

I've thought of Cindy a few times since my own cancer diagnosis. I admire how she didn't want to make a big deal about her illness and how she didn't let it keep her from achieving her dreams. After her six-game run, Cindy did an interview with our show's producers. I thought I'd share that with you:

I started watching *Jeopardy!* in the eighties. I remember when I was in ninth grade I tried out for the Teen Tournament. And I didn't pass the written exam. This year there was the in-person interview in Oklahoma City. That was really nerve-racking. I was very nervous, even though it was just a practice game. I had no idea what it would be like. I had no idea that board was that huge. Seeing what it's really like in person has been phenomenal, and it's been fun.

There were no runaway games, so I couldn't just relax. As a result it was pretty stressful each time. Even when you think the odds are completely against you, somehow via luck or something, things can work out.

I wanted to donate a lot of the money to cancer research, partly because . . . Sorry, this is hard . . . Maybe I should pause or something like that . . . but I'm dying of cancer. And I would really like the money that I win to be used to help others. So this seems like a good opportunity.

I am completely blown away by the people who showed up. My boyfriend came from Texas, and my brother flew from Sacramento, and my mom flew all the way from Virginia. It's really wonderful to see their faces. I'm just overwhelmed by the amount of support that they've shown me. It's really touching. It's been an unreal experience.

Cindy made good on her desire to help others suffering from cancer. She won approximately $100,000, which she donated to the Cancer Research Institute. Had she survived, Cindy would have appeared in the next year's Tournament of Champions. In her honor, we made a donation to that charity in the amount that tournament participants are guaranteed . . . and the remaining tournament contestants all chose to wear ribbons in support of cancer awareness on Cindy's behalf.

Who Is . . .

DANA VENATOR?

People often ask me what are the wildest things contestants have said on *Jeopardy!* David Letterman even asked me this when I was a guest on his show in 1990. That was my first appearance on David's show, and we had a lot of fun ribbing each other. He listed all the shows I hosted before *Jeopardy!*, including the short-lived ones like *Battlestars* and *Double Dare*, and said: "In those days, were you thinking to yourself, *What's going to become of me? Am I just going to go from one little game show to another?*" That got the audience laughing. Later I got him back when, in describing the process for becoming a *Jeopardy!* contestant, I said, "If you pass the test and have personality, you might wind up on the program. If you have no personality at all, you could wind up doing a talk show." The audience *really* loved that line.

David then asked about the most amusing interactions I've had with contestants. I told him about one woman in a seniors tournament who was a forensic pathologist in New York.

"What do you do in that job?" I asked.

"We examine tissue to find out what kind of disease is there," she said.

"You don't deal with me if I'm alive, right?" I said.

"No, Alex," she said, "I won't touch you if you're alive."

A high school junior from Decatur, Georgia . . .

To which I replied: "You're not the only woman to have said that to me."

I got a good laugh from our studio audience with that line, but sometimes the shoe was on the other foot. One contestant was a psychiatrist who specialized in dream interpretation. Great! I figured I'd get a free mini-consultation. I told her about a recurring dream of mine in which I am always being chased—by evil men, ogres, monsters, you name it.

"But what's unusual about all these dreams," I said, "is that they never catch me. No matter how many times they chase me, they never catch me. What does that mean?"

Her response: "It means you're a fast runner."

Kudos to the contestant. But that's not my favorite interview, either. My favorite was Dana Venator.

Dana participated in our Teen Tournament in 1987. She was a junior from Briarcliff High School in Decatur, Georgia. There are so many positive things I could say about every teenager who has played in those Teen Tournaments, but there's only one I could describe as "beginning bagpiper," and that was Dana. She was just learning how to play the instrument, and she would trudge deep into the woods behind her house to practice, so that she didn't disturb her neighbors. I just thought that was so wonderful. She also wrote short stories and what she called "bad poetry." I asked her for an example, and she recited:

Roses are red
Violets are blue
Some poems rhyme
And some don't.

She had another that she titled "The Life of a Dorito," though she refrained from sharing that one. What I found most endearing about her interview was how giddy and wide-eyed she was about the entire *Jeopardy!* experience. She seemed so tickled by every aspect.

"What's the most notable memory you're going to take back to Georgia with you?" I asked her.

"Our hotel room," she said. "It's a very nice hotel room. We took pictures of it."

That cracked me up.

"Is it that good?" I asked.

"Yeah," she said. "We're gonna buy the robe and everything."

That might have been the hardest I've ever laughed on the show. Dana has always served as a great reminder to me to never take anything for granted and to always appreciate even the simplest things.

The players I have highlighted in the last three chapters— Eddie, Cindy, and Dana—represent the best and the brightest of America, the achievers. However, I would feel remiss if I did not also acknowledge the other side of the coin, those who are not so intellectual, but who, nevertheless contribute so much to the success of our country. Many of these people are easily led or manipulated into positions of deep bias. Others feel victimized, and they are right. It is important for the rest of us to reach out to these people, to give them a voice, and most importantly to listen to that voice. Only then will we be able to bring about a reconciliation that will help mend the great chasm that divides us. And if we are really lucky, we might also resurrect an old adage that has not been heard very often in recent years: "Good politics is the art of compromise."

The Answer Is . . .

COMFORT

There are several reasons why I think *Jeopardy!* became so popular. One, I suspect, is that audiences view it with a bit more respect than other games shows. I've always said, "You never have to apologize for admitting that you watch *Jeopardy!*" The viewers feel they're getting value from the show. They're learning.

Of course, the show's longevity helps. The show was on for ten years, from 1964 to 1974. It came back for six months in 1978. And now we've been on the air for thirty-six more years. Combined, that's almost a half-century that *Jeopardy!* has been on television. And back when it debuted, it would air on NBC back-to-back with *The Hollywood Squares* between 11:00 a.m. and noon. A lot of young kids at home and college students would watch the show on their lunch breaks. They grew up with it. So when we brought it back in 1984, they were nostalgic for it. And then they raised their own kids on the show.

Another explanation for the show's popularity is that Americans are so very competitive. It's almost primal.

"I can throw the ball farther than you."

"I can run faster than you."

"No, you can't. Prove it."

Cutting the cake with Harry Friedman in celebration
of our seven thousandth show.

The day in 2005 we received a Guinness World Record for
most Emmy Awards won by a game show. At the time the
number was twenty-five. We now have thirty-five.

That competition exists within families too. Brothers and sisters. Children and parents. And grandparents—we have material that probably only grandparents, people of that generation, may know the correct response to. The information is a little arcane, a little out of the mainstream for the kids. And vice versa. There's information regarding pop culture that the parents and grandparents don't know. So there's something for everybody. And for one or two moments—and you only need a couple of moments—these opportunities to shine exist on our program. That makes you feel good about yourself and inspires a little bit of awe in the other members of the family who maybe never looked at you as being particularly sharp. "Grandpa's old and he's crotchety, but damn he knows a lot about geography!"

But I think the biggest reason the show has endured is the comfort that it brings. Viewers have gotten used to having me there, not so much as a showbiz personality but as an uncle. I'm part of the family more than an outside celebrity who comes into your home to entertain you. They find me comforting and reassuring as opposed to being impressed by me. It's not that kind of thing. I'm a second-tier celebrity. The comfortability aspect, I think, is very important. I really think that.

Viewers come to the show because it is very familiar to them. They know what to expect. They don't have to wrestle with figuring out how it works. Because we've been on for thirty-six years, it's now unlikely that a man will appear in the back of the audience in a conference room at a New York hotel and say, "Who are you?" The show has become part of the fabric of American life. People say to me, "My mother doesn't want us to call her from seven to seven thirty when *Jeopardy!* is on." Or "We have dinner with you every night."

At some point—and it occurred slowly over the years—we made the transition from just being an enjoyable quiz show to being part of your daily life. There's something ritualistic about it. It's special but not in a big way. It's not "I *must* watch *Jeopardy!*" It's "Hey, *Jeopardy!*'s on. Let's watch." It's a quality program. If it were in your pantry, it would be on the shelf labeled "Staples."

But it's not like we were an overnight sensation. We had to pay our dues. It took time. Even after we finally caught on, we were always number two in syndication behind *Wheel of Fortune*. Now we're ahead of them. It only took us thirty-six years.

What Is . . .

A MUSTACHE?

I grew the mustache toward the end of my time in Canada, not long before I came to California. Honestly, I can't remember why. I'd say it was because it was in style, but it wasn't—at least not in my industry. I was the first game show host since Groucho Marx to be on the air with a mustache. Maybe it was my rebellious streak. I have naturally wavy hair, but throughout most of my career at the CBC, they would straighten it. The hairdresser would come in each week and put the part in my hair and yank it straight. It was the mid-sixties, and they wanted me to look squeaky clean. Once the seventies came along, I started to let my hair grow longer. It got fluffier and turned into an Afro. Once I grew the mustache, I looked like Dr. J.

When I flew to LA to shoot the pilot for *The Wizard of Odds*, I walked into the NBC studio and the executive producer, Burt Sugarman, came up to me and said, "I like the mustache."

And then I ran into a doubtful-looking Lin Bolen, who was head of daytime programming for NBC.

"How do you feel about your mustache?" she asked.

"Very strongly," I said.

"Oh," she said. "Okay."

And that was the end of that. They did cut some of my hair down. But they left me with my mustache.

I wore that mustache for nearly thirty years. Then, in 2001, I decided to shave it. It was pure whim. We were about to tape our fifth and final show of the day. I went into the makeup room, sat in the chair, and I said, "I'm gonna shave my mustache." I grabbed the clippers and a razor and shaved half of it. Then one of my producers came in, and he was dumbstruck.

"Do you want me to come out with half?" I asked.

"No, no," he said. "Not half."

So I shaved the other half, and I walked out. Half the people in the audience didn't notice right away. I got the same reaction when I came home. I walked into the house. Jean was there in the Play-Doh Room with Matthew and Emily. I stood in the doorway.

"Hi, guys," I said.

"Hi, Dad," the kids responded.

"Did you have a good day taping?" Jean asked.

"Yeah, it was fine."

We talked for a few minutes . . . and a few minutes more . . . and a few minutes more.

Finally, I said, "Anyone notice anything different about Dad?"

"Oh my God," Jean said. "You shaved your mustache."

Matthew, who was around ten, started to cry. It was such a big shock. You do not mess with your children's lives in that way.

What amazed me afterward was the amount of press that got. It made newspapers and magazines everywhere. I was surprised and to a certain extent appalled by this.

Hey, I thought, *this is a television quiz show host shaving his*

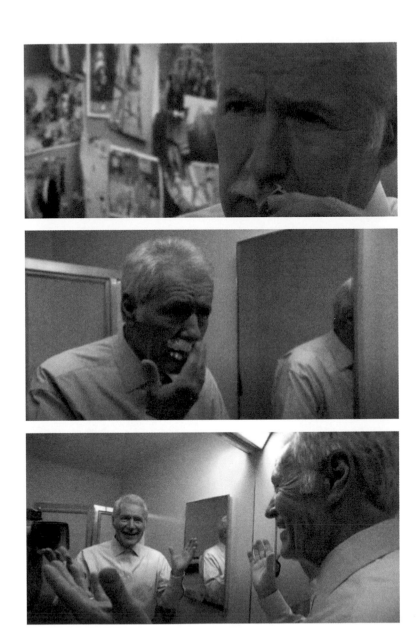

The metamorphosis.

mustache. Look at all the tragedy and calamity going on in the world. And they're asking about my mustache? Sometimes our values are a little off.

I was without a mustache from 2001 until 2014. I grew it back, and then we had our viewers vote on whether I should keep it. They voted I should shave it off again. Not everyone was in favor of this. I was a guest on *The Howard Stern Show* shortly after shaving it off that second time. Jimmy Kimmel was also a guest on the show that day.

"It was a betrayal," he said of the first time I shaved the mustache. "I actually filed a class-action lawsuit against you."

Howard said he found the mustache to be comforting. Perhaps that was always part of the appeal for viewers. During tapings, the audience still always asks: "Are you going to grow it back? When are you going to grow it back?"

Unsurprisingly, it's usually guys with mustaches themselves who pose the question.

On summer vacation a couple of years ago, I decided I would regrow the mustache. But then things got a little out of hand. Those hairs kept attracting friends. Soon I had a full-blown beard. Once again, we put the vote to fans on whether I should keep it. The winner was . . . my wife, Jean. She voted for me to be clean-shaven.

The very short-lived beard experiment.

Making a cameo on Will Ferrell's last *Jeopardy!* sketch.

Eugene Levy as me on *SCTV*.

Who Are . . .

WILL FERRELL AND
EUGENE LEVY?

Studio audiences always ask me what I think of Will Ferrell's impression of me on *Saturday Night Live*. I loved it. I even appeared on his very last Celebrity *Jeopardy!* sketch before he left *SNL*. It was a lot of fun, but to be honest, my favorite impersonation of me would be the one done by Eugene Levy on *SCTV*. They did a marvelous parody of *Reach for the Top* called *High Q*. Eugene played me. He looked more the part than Will did. He had the dark bushy hair and the black mustache. The first couple of times they did it, he was introduced as Alex Trebel. And then I guess they decided, "Let's forget about this charade. Let's just call him Alex Trebek." John Candy, Martin Short, Catherine O'Hara, Dave Thomas, and other cast members played the students. They were so stupid, and it was so funny. I never got to see it when it was originally broadcast. It took about four or five years after I left Canada for somebody to send me a tape, a compilation of all of their bits. I looked at them all at once and I thought, *My gosh, these guys are so bright.*

In a way, being parodied means you've arrived. If a comedian decides to do a takeoff of you, it's a sign that they believe their audience will immediately recognize who they are poking fun at. And if that's the case, that must mean there are a lot of people who have watched your show over the years or are watching now. They know immediately what the reference is. So you're popular not only because of your own show but because of the takeoffs and the mentions on other shows.

And it applies to other people as well. Larry King was in one of our early Celebrity *Jeopardy!* tournaments. I ran into him a few years later and he said, "I'm on the air five days a week, an hour each day, and I can't tell you how many people come up to me and say, 'Oh, I saw you on *Jeopardy!*'"

Of course, I've appeared as myself in a number of TV shows and movies, such as *Cheers, Mama's Family, The Simpsons, The X-Files, Orange Is the New Black, White Men Can't Jump,* and *The Bucket List.* I even had the honor of joining Stephen Colbert in a flying sleigh as he signed off from *The Colbert Report* for the last time. Those opportunities are always fun, though I wish someone would offer me a part that wasn't a quiz show host. I'd love it if someone came to me and said, "We'd love to cast you as an ax murderer."

There was actually a time when I thought of maybe leaving *Jeopardy!* to pursue a career in acting. I had thoughts of being an actor at the beginning of my career. I auditioned for a drama that the CBC was producing when I was a staff announcer. The casting director at the CBC agreed to let me try out for the part. I didn't get it, but she was complimentary. However, as I began to seriously consider making a career change, I started talking to a lot of my actor friends, and I learned what their schedules were.

"Wait a minute," I said, "I'm making more money than you and I work two days a week. You work six days a week, fourteen-hour days. I'm fine, thank you very much."

Appearing on *Cheers* with America's favorite know-it-all mailman, Cliff Clavin (played by John Ratzenberger), in 1990.

One of my multiple appearances on *The Simpsons*.

Watch the drool, Colbert.

Giving my best Trojan pose at USC.

What Are . . .

THE COLLEGE CHAMPIONSHIPS?

One of my favorite parts of *Jeopardy!* has been going out on the road occasionally to record the College Championships on campuses across the country. Instead of taping the show in front of two hundred people in Culver City, we're doing it in front of thousands of people in an arena. There's always the added excitement of the rivalries, such as USC versus UCLA or Michigan versus Ohio State. They're good-natured rivalries but rivalries nonetheless. The students in the audience will be cheering as if it were a sporting event.

One of the biggest laughs I ever got was when we visited the Ohio State University (where we definitely learned that it is properly referred to as *the* Ohio State University). During one of the commercial breaks, I was talking to the audience and taking questions. Most of the questions were what I typically got from audiences: what do I think makes a good contestant, or what I do think of Will Ferrell's *Saturday Night Live* impersonation. Then a young lady raised her hand.

"Yes?" I asked.

"Boxers or briefs?" she said.

That got a big laugh. Then everyone quieted down to hear my answer. I looked at her with great seriousness.

"Thong," I said.

That got an even bigger laugh.

What Is . . .

CELEBRITY *JEOPARDY!*?

It's no great secret that the material for Celebrity *Jeopardy!* is easier than in regular games. Many celebrities who appear on the show are not die-hard fans. I'm often asked if celebrities have to take a test to appear on the show. Yes. They have to be able to spell their name correctly. Our aim is to make it easier for celebrities to appear on the show, not harder. It isn't easy getting them to come on. They don't want to embarrass themselves. They don't want to screw up an answer to a seemingly easy clue and seem dumb in front of millions of viewers. So we do as much as we can to entice them, like offering the chance to win large amounts of money that will be donated to their favorite charity and holding it in an exciting venue like Radio City Music Hall.

That said, there have been some contestants who might've held their own in regular games. Usually they come from the news media. Those folks have a good grasp of current events. The actors Michael McKean and Jodie Foster are two other fierce competitors who come to mind. However, not all actors have an easy time on the show. They are always playing a role, so it's difficult for them to be themselves. Other celebrities who I feel could definitely compete on the regular version of *Jeopardy!* would have to include Aaron

Bob Woodward, Peggy Noonan, and Tucker Carlson on a
2004 Power Players episode taped in Washington, D.C.

Rodgers, Kareem Abdul-Jabbar, Anderson Cooper, Andy Richter, and Joshua Malina.

One of my favorite Celebrity *Jeopardy!* moments was in 2004 when Bob Woodward, Peggy Noonan, and Tucker Carlson appeared in one of our Power Players shows from Washington, D.C. The writers had come up with a clue that had some potential to play well, but of course we had no idea which contestant, if any, might ring in and give the correct response. The clue read:

HE'S THE SHADOWY WATERGATE SOURCE

Peggy Noonan rang in first to say, "Who is Deep Throat?"

I then turned to Watergate investigative reporter Bob Woodward.

"Bob," I said, "we've been waiting over thirty years for this. Who *is* Deep Throat?"

"How much do I get if I answer that?" he responded.

It got a huge laugh from the savvy crowd at Constitution Hall, but no answer. It was one of the funniest moments in all my years of hosting the show.

Who Is . . .

JOHNNY GILBERT?

I hired Johnny as the announcer for *Jeopardy!* Well, technically Merv hired Johnny but on my recommendation. I first met him at a party in Hollywood. And then our paths crossed a few more times. Of course I remembered him. How could you forget a voice like that? We've been together longer than either one of our marriages, and we've never had a cross word. We don't socialize outside of work, but we get along marvelously well. We love to tease each other. I'll joke with the studio audience that Johnny was the first announcer to say, "Ladies and gentlemen, the president of the United States, Abraham Lincoln."

Johnny's a little older than me, but we both began in broadcasting in the same year. Like me, he was a game show journeyman before he got to *Jeopardy!* One of the shows he announced was *Love Connection*, which was hosted by Chuck Woolery, who was indirectly responsible for me landing the *Jeopardy!* job. It's funny how small our business is considering the millions and millions of people we reach.

Not many people know that Johnny was a singer earlier in his career, and he recorded two albums in the 1960s. Over the years, we've had categories where Johnny sings songs and contestants have to guess the artist. You really haven't lived until you've heard Johnny Gilbert's rendition of Beyoncé's "Single Ladies (Put a Ring on It)."

Taking over Johnny's emcee duties at a *Jeopardy!* holiday party.

The Answer Is . . .

THE FANS

When the coronavirus was starting to spread in America, we initially considered taping the show without a studio audience. That might not seem like that big a deal to viewers at home, but trust me: the live studio audience is integral to the success of *Jeopardy!* . . . or to any quiz show or game show, for that matter.

I remember when I hosted that disastrous show *Pitfall*. We taped that in Vancouver, and there were times in the winter when the weather was so bad that the audience couldn't make it in. The opening of that show was me standing in the audience. So we faked it. We assembled the crew in some audience seats, packed tight around me, and the camera squeezed in on us, so that a dozen people seemed like a couple hundred. And then we added in canned crowd laughter and applause. It was awful.

On extremely rare instances, we've had technical problems on *Jeopardy!* that have necessitated a long delay in taping. Eventually, we sent the audiences home and taped the remaining games without them. It's tough, because you appreciate the feedback. I, along with the contestants, feed off that energy.

I really can't say enough how grateful I am for our show's fans. I try to show that gratitude as much as possible. To me, it is not optional. I see it as a requirement of my job. I've always believed that about my work in show business. If I accept a job, I will do it to the best of my ability. Even if I wake up one day and don't feel like doing it. I believe that should be the way all people should handle themselves with regard to work. If you don't want to do interviews, if you don't want to sign autographs, don't accept the job, but once you do accept it, you owe people your best performance, your best effort. So get past your ego and just be there for the people. I don't consider it a big deal.

People who come to a taping are entitled to something special. They're seeing the show, which they see on television. But you have to give them something extra. That's why I'm constantly fielding their questions and joking with them. I want them to go home having had a good experience.

FRANK SINATRA

February 5, 1987

Dear Alex:

     A line to tell you I'm a big fan and the other night with the mention of my name, I became a big star! I thank you so much and keep up the best entertainment I've seen in years.

     Good luck and God Bless,

Frank Sinatra

P.S. It's too short!!!

Mr. Alex Trebek
Merv Griffin Prodns/"Jeopardy"
1541 No. Vine Street
Hollywood, Calif. 90028

Hand delivered

A letter from the "Chairman of the Board."

Who Is . . .

FRANK SINATRA?

I don't like to name-drop but considering at the outset of this book I said it would include the highlights of my life, it would be incomplete if I didn't include my Frank Sinatra story. I met him at a golf tournament in Palm Springs. His wife, Barbara, then mentioned to me that Frank was a fan of *Jeopardy!* She said he watched the show every night. I figured she was just being nice. Not too long after, we had a whole category devoted to him. He sent me a letter that said something to the effect of, "Thanks for making me a star." I framed that letter and hung it in my office.

Receiving the Order of Canada. Though what makes
me even more proud are these three people.

What Is . . .

THE "WARM BATH" PHILOSOPHY?

In 2007, I was interviewed by the Television Academy about my career. One of the questions they asked was, "What is your proudest professional achievement?" As I told them, I have no idea. When I received the Order of Canada, I was very moved. In part, because of the other people who were receiving the award at the same time. They weren't just entertainers. It was an impressive group. But I have never thought about my life in those terms. I just enjoy the moment I'm in. For me, life is a whole experience, not just a series of isolated moments. It's like submerging yourself into a warm bath rather than sticking your toe under the faucet. It's the totality of life.

Clowning around in the costume department of
New York's Metropolitan Opera for
a Halloween-themed category in 2015.

The Answer Is . . .

SILLINESS

Jeopardy! is a fairly serious show. It's a quiz show, not a game show. There is a big difference between the two. And so as a host, you want to inject it with some levity once in a while. Not so much that you interfere with the flow. I might have already said this, and I'll probably say it again before this book is through, but it should never be about the host. Every moment you focus on yourself is a moment that you're taking away from the contestants. A few seconds in which you turn the attention on yourself might take away the time for two or three more clues, and that might change the outcome of the game. However, that doesn't mean you can't come up with humorous tidbits from time to time. It's a delicate balancing act.

Over the last decade or so, people have said to me that I've softened a little compared to the show's early days. They give the credit to Jean. They say, "After you got married, you seemed more friendly." I don't disagree with them. Jean has absolutely made me a better person. I've always had the reputation of appearing aloof. I don't know why. I think part of it is that when contestants miss a response, my job is to tell the world the correct answer, so I may come off as a know-it-all. I'm reserved to a certain extent, but I'm also silly. I think more people should include silliness as part of their daily routines.

What Is . . .

A WISH FULFILLED?

In May 1993, I made a passing mention on the show that it had always been a fantasy of mine to conduct an orchestra. I quickly got invitations from several orchestras. I settled on the Greenville Symphony Orchestra in Greenville, Pennsylvania. Greenville is a small town about an hour north from Pittsburgh. At the time it had about six thousand residents. I chose it because the orchestra was struggling to pay its bills and because I thought it seemed like a nice little weekend getaway for me and Jean.

I must admit I was nervous. My hands trembled as I tried to fasten the boutonniere on my tux. It was a sixty-seven-piece orchestra, and I was leading them in the overture to Gioachino Rossini's *Cinderella*, which isn't easy even for an experienced conductor. I don't read music, so I memorized the entire piece. And there were seventeen hundred people in attendance. But I was expertly coached by the symphony's normal conductor, Paul Chenevey, and I got a good piece of advice from one of the players. They said, "If you mess up, what are they going to do? Fire you?" That calmed me down.

Just like with *Jeopardy!* studio audiences, I opened the festivities with a joke. I said, "This is the first time I've come to a place outside Los Angeles where I did not have to be confronted with, 'Oh, there's the host of *Jeopardy!*, Pat Sajak!'"

We sold $40,000 worth of tickets, and the audience seemed to enjoy it, though I did make one unconventional choice. I conducted without a baton. I believe that's something you have to earn.

No matter how much experience I've had in front of crowds, I was very nervous for this job.

The Answer Is . . .

SLEEPING NUDE

In the summer of 2011, Jeanie and I went to San Francisco for a couple of nights. I was hosting the National Geographic World Championship at Google headquarters, and instead of me scooting up there and coming home immediately afterward, we figured we'd make a little vacation out of it.

We stayed at a very nice hotel, and we went to bed early so we could wake up first thing and do some sightseeing before I had to head to the job. I'm a light sleeper, and around 2:30 a.m. something roused me. I saw a figure walking past the foot of the bed. At first, I thought maybe I was dreaming. Then I thought it might be Jean. But I looked over and Jean was sound asleep next to me.

Hold on a minute, I thought. *If Jean is here, then who is that?*

I jumped up and put on a pair of shorts. As I did, I noticed my wallet and bracelet were missing from the dresser top where I'd put them. I hurried into the hall and saw a woman duck into the ice-machine room. I waited just outside, and when she emerged I confronted her.

"What were you doing in my hotel room?" I asked.

"I wasn't in your hotel room," she said.

"Then what are you doing up here?"

"I was visiting friends," she said.

"At two thirty in the morning? Let me call security."

At that, she took off running, and I took off after her. I got about twenty feet and just like that—*snap*. I dropped to the ground. A torn Achilles tendon. I knew it immediately.

I managed to get up and limp over to a phone by the elevators to call security. I described the woman, and they quickly apprehended her. She was arrested and eventually charged with felony first-degree burglary. Because she already had several convictions for hotel burglary, she could have faced a sentence of twenty-five years to life under California's three-strikes law. She pleaded guilty and was sentenced to seven years in prison.

I still went through with my hosting duties that day, though I had to be rolled into the auditorium in a wheelchair and use crutches to hobble around. I joked to the audience, "You're going to be tempted to blurt out responses. If you do, I will have to chase you out. Ha-ha."

There was a lot of news coverage of the event. The media made a big deal out of me sleeping in the buff. Matt Lauer even mentioned it on the *Today* show, saying, "I think we are learning a bit more than we want to know about Trebek's sleeping habits." But actually, I had a T-shirt on.

The Answer Is . . .

AN EXPENSIVE
HAIRPIECE

One of the side effects of chemotherapy is that my hair has fallen out. So ever since I started undergoing treatment, I've been wearing a hairpiece. Clearly, it's a damn good one if you didn't realize it until just now. But here's a secret even the most die-hard *Jeopardy!* fan might not know: I actually started wearing a hairpiece in early 2018, about a year before I made my initial announcement about the cancer diagnosis.

It all started one night up at the house we used to own on Lake Nacimiento in Paso Robles, a three-and-a-half-hour drive from Los Angeles. I was standing at the bathroom sink washing my face, and I lost my balance—I guess when I lifted my head up from the sink. I fell backward about six or seven feet into the tub. My ass landed on the front edge, and my head banged on the back edge. I slammed into the tub so hard it moved about an eighth of an inch.

I didn't black out, and I wasn't bleeding, so I went back to bed and woke up the next morning figuring everything was fine. Well, soon I started having these episodes where I'd lose my balance. I would start to tip over and then quickly right myself. Some people thought I was doing it intentionally, just kidding around, trying to get a laugh. But it started happening more often. And my left leg started to drag a little. When I got to work one morning, Tad, our security guy, said, "You gotta a little hitch in your giddyup."

"Yeah," I said. "I've noticed that."

Going around corners, I would bump into the wall. My spatial awareness was all out of whack.

Around this same time, I had an annual physical scheduled at Cedars-Sinai.

"Everything okay?" my doctor asked.

"Yeah," I said. "But I've got this little thing when I'm walking— this hitch."

He asked me to step off the table, and I sort of missed a step.

"Were you just having fun with me?" he asked. "Or was that for real?"

"Yeah," I said. "That's one of these things I was telling you about."

"Okay," he said, "you're going over to emergency."

"Oh shit," I said.

By this point, I'd been to the Cedars-Sinai emergency room so many times over the years I was practically on a first-name basis with staff. There were numerous handyman-incurred bumps and bruises, kidney stones, and not one but two heart attacks. (I've had so many maladies we turned them into a *Jeopardy!* category. When we revealed it in the game, it got a big laugh from the studio audience.)

For that first heart attack, I didn't want to go to the hospital. Jeanie insisted.

"Something's wrong," she said. "You've gotta go *now*."

I never use my status as a public figure to get preferential

THE MEDICAL FILE OF ALEX TREBEK

At least something good came of all my health woes: we got a category out of it.

treatment. I certainly don't cut lines. Not at movies or restaurants or anywhere else. I've always resented people who pull that crap. I'm not like Gordon MacRae at the Brown Derby all those years ago. I'm happy to stand in line quietly and wait my turn. But you say the words *heart attack* in a hospital and you don't have a choice. Then you're in like a shot.

I was worried, but not because it might be a heart attack. I was worried because it might *not* be. They started connecting me to the machines and speaking their jargon.

"MI?" I asked. "Is that a myocardial infarction?"

"Yes," the nurse said.

"That's a heart attack, right?" I asked.

"Yes," she said.

"Oh, thank God," I said.

"Why are you saying that?" she asked.

"I didn't want to come here and waste your time," I told her.

I mean, if you go into the hospital and say, "I think I'm having a heart attack," and they zip you to the front of the line and go to the trouble of running all those tests and it turns out not to be a heart attack? You have to feel pretty embarrassed.

Well, I had the same worry that day my doctor sent me to the ER because of my balance issues. I was worried it was going to turn out to be nothing. They ran an MRI on my brain, and when they came back with it, they were all smiling.

"Good news," they said. "It's not a stroke."

"Oh, great," I said.

"The bad news," they said, "is that you have major blood clots on both sides of your brain . . . bilateral subdural hematoma."

"Damn," I said.

"We have to remove them," they said.

"Can we do it now?" I asked.

"Have you eaten?" they asked.

"Yeah," I said.

"It's okay," they said. "We'll do it first thing in the morning."

The next day at five in the morning, they did the surgery. On my cell phone I still have two pictures Jeanie took of my skull afterward. I don't save any photos on my phone. I barely save any numbers. But these two I kept. There were long stitches on each side of my scalp where they cut through the skull in order to flush out both sides properly. These two rows of stitches look like a railway track. And in between the railway track is this flimsy tuft of gray hair hanging there. It was like a reverse Mohawk.

It scared the crap out of the staff when I went in. It wasn't looking too good. That's when the producers decided I needed a hairpiece to cover it and our experience with the hairpiece started.

The guy who did it does wigs for a lot of the big stars, mostly women. I won't share their names, but I bet you'd be surprised. I certainly was. These pieces are so good. Nobody can tell. After I announced my cancer diagnosis I sat down for an interview with Jane Pauley on *CBS Sunday Morning*. She was totally shocked when I told her it was a hairpiece, and she was sitting two feet away from me.

I usually let the makeup team at work put it on, but in a pinch I can do it myself. I did it once when Jeanie and I went out to dinner, and it wasn't bad. In my case the hairpiece makes me look better than my real hair. I probably should've started wearing it a long time ago.

Real hair or hairpiece? To be honest, I'm not sure myself.

What Is . . .

TOUGHNESS?

There are moments when I have some regrets about having gone public with my diagnosis. Because I have become in many ways the de facto spokesperson for pancreatic cancer, there are a lot of expectations, a lot of people looking to me for reassurance. I feel a lot of pressure to always be tough—to be stoic and show a stiff upper lip. But I'm a goddamn wuss. I start to cry for no reason at all. I have no idea what sets it off, and it embarrasses me.

The thought that I don't measure up compared to people's expectations is difficult. You can go back to the notion of courage and bearing the burden of the situation. The burden of the cancer. The burden of the treatment. Am I bearing it well or am I a coward? It doesn't make me feel good to think that way. I'd like to be a noble leader. I'd like to be El Cid. I know that's how others see me: as this compelling, brave leader. Not long ago, when I was going through a significant bout of depression, I called my doctor and expressed my concern about not being strong enough.

"No, no, no," he said, trying to reassure me. "You're a great survivor. You've helped a lot of people. You don't know how many people whose lives you have saved just by being out there, speaking out about the disease, what it does to you, and how to maintain a more positive attitude."

That helped pick my spirits up somewhat, but that's not the way I see myself. Because I think a lot of people are going through stuff that's worse than mine.

I remember in the early 1990s I was in Washington, D.C., doing some work for World Vision. The subject of AIDS came up. Now, in those days we didn't know much about AIDS. We didn't know much about how it was transmitted. Magic Johnson had just been diagnosed with HIV, and Karl Malone and several other NBA players expressed concern about playing against him for fear of contracting the virus. It was a scary time. That day in Washington, I was told about a house where they were sheltering a number of AIDS patients. Somebody asked me if I was interested in going to the house.

"Yeah," I said. "Let's go."

There were about a dozen men in different conditions. Some of them had lots of sores on their bodies. All of them were thin. I went in and started exchanging conversations with them. I shook hands with them. I hugged them. I spent the better part of an hour with them. They seemed grateful for my visit, and I left hoping that I had done some good.

There are a lot of people out there who have cancer and other illnesses who continue to live their lives and go about their business, and they do it without recognition. I'm in the public eye, so I get a lot of recognition because of that. But it does place some responsibility on me that I feel I'm not deserving of.

Interestingly, the longer I've lived with the cancer, the more my definition of *toughness* has changed. I used to think not crying meant you were tough. Now I think *crying* means you're tough. It means you're strong enough to be honest and vulnerable. It means you're not pretending. And not pretending, being willing to let your guard down and show people how you truly feel and admit that you're a wuss, is one of the toughest things a person can do.

It's also one of the most helpful things a person can do. Because sharing your feelings with others brings people closer together. It demonstrates an interest in developing an understanding. It demonstrates a caring. Because you have to figure there are some people out there who are going through the same stuff. A friend's wife was recently diagnosed with cancer and is experiencing a lot of the same things that I've been going through. She's experiencing pain. She's experiencing fatigue. She's experiencing depression. And I say, "Oh, thank God I'm not the only one!" If you're able to, you should share your experiences so that people out there can say, "I'm not alone. There's somebody else going through the same thing, and they're bearing up well. Maybe I can also." If that's a way for you to inspire people, then there is a lot of merit in that.

There is nothing worse than deluding yourself and trying to make yourself out to be somebody you're not—somebody you're not comfortable being. There's nothing wrong with having foibles. There's nothing wrong with saying, "I'm really depressed today, and I have no idea why. Why am I crying?" There's nothing wrong with a man shedding a tear.

My quarantine uniform now that I'm not wearing a suit at work.

What Is . . .

THE WILL TO SURVIVE?

On that trip to Bosnia and Herzegovina with the USO, I was driven through Kosovo. All of the homes and apartment buildings were just blasted to bits. And yet there was one big five-story apartment building on one corner, and the troops who were escorting me said, "That building is special. On one floor there is an elderly couple living there. They are the only ones living there." They had survived, and they were still staying in their apartment, and no one dared bother them.

The will to survive is so strong in many people. You see it in tragedies all the time, whether it's earthquakes, tornados, hurricanes, or floods. The people who live, the people who survive, we say, "My God, how did they get through that?" Well, there's a will to survive, and there's a lot of luck and a lot of God's help that comes into play.

I don't think the will to survive is a constant. I think there are moments—and there are certainly moments in my life—when that will to survive disappears and I'm ready to pack it in. Because I understand that death is part of life. And I've lived a long life. If I were in my twenties with years ahead of me, I might feel differently. But when you're about to turn eighty it's not like you're missing out on a great many things. The will to survive is there, and then you get hit with shock waves—whether pain or unpredicted surges of depression or just debilitating moments of agony, weakness. I don't have much stamina anymore. It's not even a question of physical activity that tires me out. Just being awake is enough to exhaust me. Some days are better than others. I had a couple of good days, then yesterday didn't go so well. Today is fair. Just pain and fatigue and, well, different kinds of agony. Each day brings a new set of challenges. One day the pain is on my right side at the back, the other day it's in my stomach, the other day it's down in my lower abdomen. It gets sharp, lasts fifteen minutes, and then goes away. It's very capricious.

The chemo treatment is no fun either. It affects my mind as well as my body. I know no one in our circle of friends who keeps losing things as often as I do. I mean, I was at the dinner table the other night and I said, "Where's Jeanie?" My wife was sitting right next to me. That's not a good sign. Jean says it's likely the drugs, but that's the kind of story that people who have cancer will relate to—these little moments of delirium where you don't know what the hell's going on.

One of the things I've discovered throughout the process with pancreatic cancer and the chemo is that nothing seems to last. The great pain and all of the other things are short-lived. And thank God for that, because if they were constant, that's when you'd fall into despair and you'd give up and you'd terminate your life or you allow your life to pass. And I've had letters from people about that. They've given up. They're not doing the chemo. They're just dealing with the pain.

For each person it is a different experience. I've gotten letters from people who say they've been going through treatment for ten years. They are survivors, and they're committed to continuing. And I've also heard from people who've decided to stop treatment and just manage to do palliative care until they die. One man lasted only three days. It's a personal choice, and that choice doesn't make you more or less brave than someone else. Sometimes there's a lot to be said for dying.

I don't like to use the terms *battling* or *fighting* when talking about cancer. It suggests that there are only two outcomes: "winning" and "losing." If you don't get well, then you are a "loser." If you have decided to stop treatment, you have "given up." That's nonsense.

I understand why we human beings choose to see cancer in these terms. It's easier to comprehend and less scary if we see the experience as a boxing match and the disease as an opponent who might be subdued by sheer force of will and determination. However, cancer doesn't get demoralized. It doesn't require a pep talk from its trainer between rounds. It is a fight, that's true. There are days when I feel like Mike Tyson just dropped to the canvas by a Buster Douglas uppercut. But it is by no means a fair fight. Not even close. It is simple biology. You get treatment and you get better. Or you don't. And neither outcome is an indication of your strength as a person.

Yet I still believe in the will to live. I believe in positivity. I believe in optimism. I believe in hope, and I certainly believe in the power of prayer.

Jean's bathroom remodel, before and after.

What Is . . .

PROBLEM-SOLVING?

As I've said before, I enjoy solving problems. That's why I love working around the house. There was a photo that went viral not too long ago of me in the floorboards of my wife's bathroom. I had decided I was going to redo her bathroom the way she wanted it done. The one thing she really wanted was a soaking tub, which meant removing the old Jacuzzi tub. That was an ordeal. It was cast-iron covered in porcelain. We had to cut it in three pieces because it was so big and heavy we couldn't get it out. We used a Sawzall, a metal cutter, and a torch, and we finally got the damn thing out. Before we brought in the soaking tub, I thought it would be smart to reinforce the floor. So I went down into the crawl space under her bathroom and then realized I had to readjust the floor joists in order to accommodate the incoming waterlines. And it wound up looking pretty good. We show the before and after photos to studio audiences, and their reaction is very positive. Jeanie picked out all the tiles and fixtures. I stayed out of that part.

Our garage is a three-car garage that can't fit any cars because it's so crammed with tools. Another question the audience will ask me is "Is it true you bought a hardware store?" No, I did not buy the store. But I did buy just about everything inside of it. There was this hardware store in the San Fernando Valley that was going out of business, so I bought a lot of its inventory. I have tons of tools and things I don't even know what they are or what they're used for. One of them I've been wondering about for years is a Woodruff key. Go look it up. I'm equipped to handle almost any project. I have a lot of drills. I have a lot of saws. I have enough screwdrivers of all types to last a lifetime even if I lost one every week. I have some pieces of specialty equipment I've only used once, such as a propane tank with a burner attachment for repairing torch-down roofing material. But if I get a leak I can drag that sucker onto the roof and do my thing. I've also become very adept at walking on Spanish roof tiles without cracking them.

It isn't just heavy-duty projects that interest me. Right now, for instance, I'm working on replacing a cover over an outdoor swing and I've been having the damnedest time with that thing. I'm using a portable sewing machine that Jeanie bought me. I'm not unfamiliar with sewing machines. My mother had two: an electric one and a very old Singer treadle machine. This machine is top-of-the-line, but it's causing me problems. It works for a while, then it jams. And then it works. And then it jams. And sometimes I mess up.

So far I've sewn the same strip of material three times incorrectly. *Three times.* Finally, I ripped open the seams and tore the fabric. So what was going to be a five-inch flap is now a four-and-a-half-inch flap, because I had to sew back behind the cuts in the fabric that were errors.

I'm going to get it done, and it will look okay. It won't look great. But I will have accomplished it, and it's something I've never done before. It's challenging, and that's part of what makes life so special: when challenges come up that you've never experienced before.

That's very important in life. It's one thing to be able to do the same thing well over and over again. But try to force yourself into attacking a new project that you've never done before, and say, "Okay, how do I solve this?"

I can fix a lot of the mechanical things. I can't fix electronics. I don't have the testing equipment to determine whether the circuits are gone. Some appliances I can handle. I did repair the clothes dryer when it wasn't working. First, I called a repair guy and had him come over.

"It's gonna cost two hundred dollars," he said.

"*What?*" I said. I thought about just replacing the whole unit. But then I looked up what part it was, and eventually I installed it. And it worked. It's a question of paying attention. I mean, if these technicians can do it, why the hell can't I? That's always been my attitude. "If this guy can repair this plumbing leak, why can't I? If he can solder this copper pipe, why can't I? It ain't that complex."

I know what you're thinking: a plumbing leak is one thing. But why would he spend so much time and energy trying to repair the cover of an outdoor swing when he could probably purchase an entirely new swing for three hundred dollars? I admit, there have been times when I've gotten so pissed I've said, "Damn it, I'm just gonna throw this all in the garbage and buy a new one." But no, I want to prove to myself that I can do it. It's like the crossword puzzles that I keep working on. When I started doing crossword puzzles, I couldn't do them for diddly. And now I'm ticked if I don't finish them all, even the tough ones later in the week. It's a source of pride.

It's a problem. Solve it. Problem-solving is an important part of anyone's life. That mindset certainly doesn't hurt going through all this treatment for cancer.

Receiving an honorary doctorate from Fordham University (*top*);
at the University of Ottawa (*bottom*).

The Answer Is . . .

EDUCATION

Curiosity has always been a very important factor in my life—about all subjects. It's a thirst for knowledge. I have a standard motto and it's very short: "A good education and a kind heart will serve you well throughout your entire life." The more you know, the more knowledge you acquire, the better off you are in dealing with other people—the more you develop an *understanding* for other people.

If you know geography, for instance, you learn why a certain civilization settled in one location as opposed to another location twenty miles away. They settled *here* because they discovered there was salt in the ground. They settled *there* because there was water and fish. There's a natural order to the way the world has become populated.

That natural order unfortunately has been overtaken by man's interference in setting up all kinds of international boundaries. We have drawn boundaries that make it difficult to achieve peace. And that's unfortunate. It's man's hubris. It's man's arrogance—that he knows best where these boundaries should be formed. Little by little we make mistakes, and we keep compounding those mistakes, and expanding on them to the point where you can't get people to agree anymore. Unfortunately, a lot of people don't take the time to educate themselves. They don't put in the effort.

As I tell studio audiences, you are never too old to learn. There's a thrill connected to curiosity. Because curiosity leads to discovery. And there's a thrill that comes with discovery. "I didn't know that! Jeez, how about that?!" Somebody on staff just gave me a copy of *National Geographic* magazine from July of 1940, which is the month in which I was born. I've got it right here on my desk and have been leafing through it. One of the main articles is about the construction of the new National Gallery of Art in Washington. And the facade, the article says, is wider than the facade of the Capitol Building. So I thought, *Boy, that's interesting. That's a pretty big building.* I also learned that the dome of the National Gallery was modeled after the Pantheon in Rome.

Now, am I ever going to use that knowledge? Probably not. But even if you are learning facts that you are not going to be able to use in your daily life, it enriches you—the fact itself just enriches you as a human being and broadens your outlook on life and makes you a more understanding and better person. And as Martha Stewart would say, "That's a good thing."

Hosting the National Geographic GeoBee.

What Is . . .

AN EMOJI? (NO, REALLY, WHAT IS IT?)

I do not have a favorite app. I use my phone for something completely revolutionary. I make a call. I receive a call. I prefer simpler things in life.

For much of my childhood, there was no television. We only had radio, motion pictures, periodicals, and books. Most of your information about the world you got from books. Now there's the internet, social media, video games. Technology is taking over the world.

There's a book sitting on my desk right now by Yuval Noah Harari called *21 Lessons for the 21st Century*. Some of his main points are about how technology and robots and AI are changing our society to the point where we need to start considering what kind of an existence we're going to have.

It's already happening. When I go on my computer to research something, those little sidebars come up. I may be researching history but something comes up on television sets or telephone systems or things that I bought to do repairs around the house. The computer knows where I've been.

I also see it with my drug prescriptions. They know when I'm running out and they renew automatically. I don't know how the hell I got ahead of them, but I've got too many pills. I take them once a day. They're supposed to last ninety days. Maybe they renew every seventy-five days. You get fifteen pills ahead each month over a period of years, that adds up.

I dazzled my wife the other day. She was out of town, and someone had sent a beautiful flower arrangement to her. I said, "Oh God, these flowers will be dead and gone by the time she gets back." So I took a picture and figured out how to send the picture to her. She sent me back a lovely message. She said, "Look at you, you're texting! And sending a picture!" And she put a heart and one of them little smiley faces at the end. I don't know how to do that yet.

With Jean in Antarctica. I don't know what I'd do without her.

The Answer Is . . .

THE CAREGIVERS

What I've discovered in all of this is how extremely difficult it is for caregivers, and for loved ones looking after those who are sick. Jean doesn't complain, but I worry about the toll it is taking on her. I worry how it's affecting Matthew and Emily too. They were so upset when I first told them the diagnosis. I know one thing that frustrates them is that I'm not as communicative as I probably should be about what I'm going through. But I'm their father. I want to shield them from any pain. I'm happy that they have lives of their own and I don't want them to see me when I'm going through an especially bad day. But now because of the COVID-19 quarantine, I can't shield them from it. And gradually they have adjusted in ways that have increased my pride in them. They're around me much more than before, and I know why. And it makes me love them even more.

Backstage, contemplating my opening remarks.

What Is . . .

RETIREMENT?

For years, studio audiences have asked me, "Have you ever thought about retiring?"

And I'll respond, "Yes, I've thought about it. Why? Do you know something I don't?"

Or they'll ask, "How do you motivate yourself to do the same job year after year?"

And I'll respond, "They pay me very well."

One of the elements of my personality has always been—and I'm keenly aware of this—that if something was that important to me, that much of a driving force, then I would do something about it. The fact that I have not done something about changing my job is an indication that maybe I'm pretty satisfied, pretty content with where I am. It's not hard to be content with being the thirty-six-year host of *Jeopardy!* You get a lot of respect. And, as I've discovered since the diagnosis revelation, you get a lot of love. There really is no downside to it. It's not like I trudge to work every week and say, "Oh gosh, I've gotta do *Jeopardy!* again."

It invigorates me. It's the strangest thing now with cancer: there are days when I'm just a basket case before we tape. I can barely walk to the production meeting. But when Johnny introduces me and I get out onstage, it all changes suddenly. I'm myself again. I feel good. One taping day early in my treatment, my stomach cramps got so bad that I was on the floor writhing in pain. My pain level went from a three to an eleven. And it happened three or four times that day. I finished taping one of the shows and just made it back to my dressing room before collapsing and crying from the pain. I had fifteen minutes before the next show.

"If you don't want to do the show, we'll just cancel taping," the producers said.

"No," I said. "We're here. We're doing the shows."

I *really* don't understand how that happens. Other people on our staff have noticed it too. It's like, "Get him off his deathbed and push him out and let him run the show and he's fine. And then bring him backstage and put him back on the cot. Put him back on the gurney until the contestants are out and ready to go for the next show."

I do not have an explanation for it. But it happens. And thank God it does. No matter how I feel before the show, when I get out there it's all forgotten because there's a show to be done. Work to do. "You know what you have to do, Trebek. Do it. Keep it moving. *Run the game.*"

Yet I know there will come a time when I won't be able to answer that bell. I know there will come a time when I can no longer do my job as host—do it as well as the job demands, as well as *I* demand. Part of it is physical. Standing on your feet for eleven hours two days in a row is difficult for someone who's about to turn eighty, even without getting worn down by chemotherapy. Several years back, Mark Goodson hired me to host a reboot of *To Tell the*

Truth, and I loved it because it was the first time in my career as a host of quiz shows and game shows that I got the chance to host a show sitting down. My, my, what a joy that was. My eyesight has also deteriorated over the years. It's not as easy for me to read the clues. The chemo has caused sores inside my mouth that make it difficult for me to enunciate. One treatment also turned my skin dark brown, and the chemo, of course, caused my hair to fall out.

But part of it is mental too. I'm the first to admit I'm not as sharp as I once was. I have more and more brain skips. What I call "senior moments." I'll transpose numbers. I'll say 1974 instead of 1947. And I won't notice I've made that mistake until the producers ask me to reread the clue. In my younger years, I would catch myself just before I was about to make a mistake and do it correctly. Later on, I would realize I had made the mistake just after I made it. Now, I don't even know I made an error. But I figure, *Hell, I've got the job . . . who cares?* I do find that the older you get, the more difficult it is to maintain your concentration. And in this job, concentration is imperative. You can have those slipups in casual conversation with friends. But you can't get away with that as the host of *Jeopardy!*

Whenever it gets to that point, I'll walk away. You won't see Johnny wheeling me out onto the stage. "Here, Alex, let me wipe that drool off your chin. Okay, now go ahead and start the game."

And *Jeopardy!* will be just fine. It doesn't matter who's the host. It's a quality program. Look at *The Price Is Right*. When Drew Carey replaced Bob Barker, so many people said the show would never survive. It's still a success. There are other hosts out there who can do equally as good a job as me. I think *Jeopardy!* can go on forever.

Sometimes it's good to take a break.

What Is . . .

GETTING YOUR
AFFAIRS IN ORDER?

I keep reading about people who have different kinds of cancer, and they see their doctor and say, "Well, what's the prognosis?" And the doctor says, "I think you better get your affairs in order." My doctor has not said that to me. He has told me he is there for me, no matter what my decision is. There are different decisions, of course. I could decide to begin a new chemotherapy protocol. I could decide to try a new immunotherapy. Or I could decide to go to hospice.

The other day, I talked to my doctor for the very first time about this last option and about what goes on. He explained that hospice is basically there to make you comfortable on your way to the end. They're not there to administer health care but palliative care.

I have also started the process of getting my finances organized for the family. I talked to my bank in Toronto this morning. I had to get up early to do it because of the time difference. I was transferring some Canadian funds into American funds.

"I hope you won't mind if I ask you a few questions to verify your identity," the bank representative said.

"Sure," I said.

"What is the name of the university that both you and I attended?"

"The University of Ottawa."

"What was your hometown?"

"Sudbury."

Then he asked something else, which I answered correctly.

"One question you haven't asked," I said. " 'Who has one of the longest-running savings accounts at the Royal Bank of Canada Yonge and Grenville branch?' "

"That was going to be my next question," he said with a laugh.

I think I got my account started in 1964. Fifty-six years with the same account at the same bank. Who has a bank account for fifty-six years? And I still don't know how to write a deposit slip correctly. Of course, now everything can be done by computer and phone— in theory, at least. But try calling your bank and getting through to a real person. There are so many hoops to jump through. It drives me nuts. Just because I'm sick and have gained some perspective on what's important doesn't mean I'm not still irritated by small stuff.

Speaking of what's important: Matthew just drove home from New York, where he co-owns two popular restaurants in Harlem. One is a Mexican restaurant called Oso and the other is a pizza place called Pizza by Lucille's. He named it after his grandmother, and he has clearly inherited his grandfather's love for the kitchen. Matthew would have flown, but for this visit, he had company . . . his dog, Luna. She had been left tied to a post outside his restaurant for six hours one night, so when no one came to claim her, he took her home and she has won over his heart. She's the most docile pit bull you ever saw.

Matt says he came home because the coronavirus had shut

down the restaurants' dining-in service. It's a good excuse, but I know the real reason why he came. He recognizes this is our last go-round. He's here to spend quality time with me before we have no time left to spend together.

Emily too has recognized the importance of spending more quality time together. Recently, just before the quarantine went into effect, she and I for the first time went to a movie, just the two of us, alone together. We had never done that before. Afterward, we talked about our relationship and the deep feelings of love and respect we have for each other. She's an amazing young woman.

This morning I sat down with her, Matt, and Jeanie, and told them I had made my decision. I'm going to stick with this current protocol, then that's it. If it doesn't work I'll probably stop treatment. It wasn't an easy conversation, and it isn't any easier writing these words. Quality of life was an important consideration.

Once we had a good cry and they had a chance to absorb the news, Matthew said to me, "Well, what about other natural-type foods? Would you be willing to try some of those?"

"It depends," I said, "but don't tell me about them. Let Mom just sneak them into my food."

And Jean said: "I've been doing that for a month and a half!"

We all had a good laugh about that.

I'm not afraid of dying. One thing they're not going to say at my funeral as part of the eulogy is "He was taken from us too soon." I'm about to turn eighty. I've lived a good, full life, and I'm nearing the end of it. I know that. The only thing that might bother me is if I pass on before I get to have grandchildren. (Hint, hint.)

But when death happens, it happens. Why should I be afraid of it? Now, if it involves physical suffering, I might be afraid of that. But, according to my doctor, that's what hospice is for.

They want to make it as easy as it can possibly be for you to transition into whatever future you happen to believe in. Am I a believer? Well, I believe we are all part of the Great Soul—what some call God. We are God, and God is us. We are one with our maker. How do I know this? It's not that I know it. It's that I *feel* it. The same way that when I go to Africa I feel that is where I came from. The same way I feel that Jean is my soul mate. I feel it in my gut.

But do I pray to a specific god? Do I anticipate a particular version of the afterlife? No, I do not. For all I know I'll wind up coming back in another life as a knitter during the French Revolution sitting there like Madame Defarge watching the executions. However, lately I've been thinking more and more about that old line they used to use in the military: "No one's an atheist in a foxhole." If ever there was an opportunity to believe in God—*a* god—this might be a good one, Trebek, now that you're on the verge. What have you got to lose?

The Answer Is . . .

LIFE

My life has been a quest for knowledge and understanding, and I'm nowhere near having achieved that. And it doesn't bother me in the least. I will die without having come up with the answer to many things in life.

I'm often asked how I would like to be remembered. I don't think about it much. That doesn't really jibe with my "warm bath" outlook on life that I mentioned earlier. But I suppose if I had to answer I would say I'd like to be remembered first of all as a good and loving husband and father, and also as a decent man who did his best to help people perform at their best. Because that was my job. That is what a host is supposed to do. You are there to make the contestants relax enough that they can demonstrate their skills. They are the stars of the show. They are the ones the viewers tuned in to see. And if you do that, if you put the focus on the players rather than on yourself, the viewers will look on you as a good guy. If that's the way I'm remembered, I'm perfectly happy with that.

After our conversation about my decision, I said to Jean and the kids, "Why don't we all go to the movies tomorrow? I will take over a theater, and we will be the only four people there, so there's little risk of infection." I know it's not going to happen but it's fun to think about. With the coronavirus, we can't go out to eat, we can't go out to public places, even the park next door has limited its use. There aren't that many things available for us to do. Here I am wanting to enjoy what might be the last of my days, and, what, I'm supposed to just stay at home and sit in a chair and stare into space?

Actually, that doesn't sound too bad. Except instead of a chair, I'll sit on the swing out in the yard. That's my favorite spot on the whole property. I used to do it with Mom. Just sit there and rock. No need to talk. The view of the yard lays out beautifully. I can see across the grass and past the driveway all the way down to my two artificial Canada geese feeding there and then even farther beyond to my ancient Roman sundial in the entry to the pool. It's just very peaceful. I fell asleep there a couple of times this week. And I finally finished sewing that damn rain cover, so I never have to sit in a puddle. The water just slides right off. I suppose the feeling I have sitting on that porch swing is similar to what people feel when they meditate, though I would never call it meditating. I just consider it goofing off, not doing anything.

Yep, I'll be perfectly content if that's how my story ends: sitting on the swing with the woman I love, my soul mate, and our two wonderful children nearby. I'll sit there for a while and then maybe the four of us will go for a walk, each day trying to walk a little farther than the last. We'll take things one step at a time, one day at a time. In fact, I think I'll go sit in the swing for a bit right now.

The weather is beautiful—the sun is shining into a mild, mild looking sky, and there's not a cloud in sight.

IMAGE CREDITS

ABOUT THE AUTHOR

ALEX TREBEK has hosted the syndicated quiz show *Jeopardy!* for thirty-six seasons, earning him seven Daytime Emmy Awards—including a Lifetime Achievement Award—and the Guinness World Record for most episodes of a game show hosted by the same presenter. Prior to *Jeopardy!*, he hosted numerous quiz shows and games shows, including *The Wizard of Odds* and *High Rollers*. He began his career with the Canadian Broadcasting Corporation, working there for more than a decade. He graduated from the University of Ottawa and holds honorary doctorates from the University of Ottawa and Fordham University. He has worked with the humanitarian organization World Vision since the early 1980s, and has contributed to various other philanthropic organizations, including the USO, UNCF, National Geographic Society, and the Hope of the Valley Rescue Mission. Originally from Sudbury, Ontario, he resides in Los Angeles with his wife, Jean.